My Praise Is Greater Than My Struggle

My Praise Is Greater Than My Struggle

By
Dr. Tiffany A. Little

XULON PRESS

Xulon Press
2301 Lucien Way #415
Maitland, FL 32751
407.339.4217
www.xulonpress.com

© 2020 by Dr. Tiffany A. Little

All rights reserved solely by the author. The author guarantees all contents are original and do not infringe upon the legal rights of any other person or work. No part of this book may be reproduced in any form without the permission of the author. The views expressed in this book are not necessarily those of the publisher.

Unless otherwise indicated, Scripture quotations taken from the Holy Bible, New International Version (NIV). Copyright © 1973, 1978, 1984, 2011 by Biblica, Inc.™. Used by permission. All rights reserved.

Scripture quotations taken from the King James Version (KJV)–*public domain.*

Printed in the United States of America.

ISBN-13: 978-1-6305-0877-7

Contents

	Introduction	*vii*
1.	Chapter One: The Plan	1
2.	Chapter Two: The Growth Mindset	15
3.	Chapter Three: The Divine Delivery	25
4.	Chapter Four: Put It Away	35
5.	Chapter Five: Positioning for God's Transformation	51
6.	Chapter Six: You've Got to Move	59
7.	Chapter Seven: Moving from Fear to Faith	72
8.	Chapter Eight: The Test	81
9.	Chapter Nine: God Chose You	101
10.	Chapter Ten: Give Thanks and Praise to God	113
11.	Chapter Eleven: Praise Reports	124

Introduction

*The voice of joy, and the voice of gladness, the voice of the bridegroom, and the voice of the bride, the voice of them that shall say, Praise the L*ORD *of hosts: for the L*ORD *is good; for his mercy endureth forever: and of them that shall bring the sacrifice of praise into the house of the L*ORD*. For I will cause to return the captivity of the land, as at the first, saith the L*ORD*.*
—Jeremiah 33:11

This book is written in memory of my mother-in-law, Fannie K. Little. She received her ultimate healing of cancer on July 6, 2012. I had the honor and the privilege of giving remarks and sharing reflections from the family at her funeral services. The following are the words and the reflections that I gave. These remarks marked the beginning of a powerful revelation for me that inspired me to write this book in her honor and for my witness to the power of God.

Reflections—My Praise Speaks Louder Than My Struggle

Mrs. Little was indeed a woman of great faith and strength. Some may wonder if she maintained this positive, optimistic, and faithful demeanor at all times, and if one person could answer this truthfully—you would think it would be me, her daughter-in-law. I am so grateful to say that for every piece of good that all of you were able to see, her children and family received it in double portions. Mrs. Little and I often praised God over the fact that we didn't have the same hurdles that other mother and daughter-in-law relationships had. While I am an okay person, this was mainly because of her spirit and willingness to share with me the most precious gift of all—her son, Fernando. I, however upped the ante and was upgraded in her eyes when I helped give her, in her own words, "handsome and precious grandboys."

When I reflect back upon Mrs. Little's faith walk, the scripture of Jeremiah 33:11 rings out to me: "the sounds of joy and gladness, the voices of bride and bridegroom, and the voices of those who bring thank offerings to the house of the LORD, saying, 'Give thanks to the LORD Almighty, for the LORD is good; his love endures forever.'" In essence, this scripture helped me realize that Mrs. Little's praises spoke louder than her struggle. There were so many examples of this just within the last three months. I know that her heart ached when her brother passed away, yet her praises were louder than her struggle. Two weeks later, her sister suffered seizures, a mild heart attack, and a possible stroke, yet her praise was louder than her struggle. Very recently, she had begun to have discomfort in her stomach, and the cancer seemed to be coming back, yet her praise spoke louder than her struggle.

When it appeared that the cancer was coming back, the doctors took a CT scan. Mrs. Little called me and said, "Fernando asked me what I thought the test results were going to say and I told him they are going to be clear." Why did she say that? Because her praise spoke louder than her struggle. In that conversation, we both said that we couldn't wait to share and report the good news, just like we did back in January when we shouted praise to God that she was cancer free, once we got those test results back. Little did I know that her faith would be to this degree and that the next

Introduction

time we would be back in church to give the report we would be at this funeral.

Now we find ourselves as her children and husband having to see if our praise can speak louder than our struggle. So, as she taught me, whenever you have a chance to witness, whenever you have a chance to let your praise speak louder than your struggle, then you have to tell what the Lord has done for the mighty and the faithful.

Church Family, I have a praise report. On Friday, the doctors said that infection and cancer had taken over her body, that she was facing liver and kidney failure, and that dialysis was needed. The doctors were telling the family to prepare for the worst and begin to make some critical decisions. However, because my husband Fernando's praise spoke louder than his struggle, he told his mom to fight as long as she wanted to fight because it would be a win-win either way. My sister-in-law Alicia's praise spoke louder than her struggle; she told her mother while she would miss her, she didn't want to see her suffer down here on earth. My father-in-law Gregory Little's praise spoke louder than his struggle. He said, "I don't want her hurting at all."

We all began to praise God, and the sounds of our praise and Mrs. Little's praises began to go up as we made our request known. God moved in a way that only He could move, and God did just what He said he was going to do. Let me tell you that on that very day God took Mrs. Little, she is now 100 percent cancer free, her liver and kidneys are completely renewed, she no longer needs dialysis, and she no longer needs to be revitalized with a machine or medicine because she has gained eternal life and has entered into the gates of the Almighty. That's why my praise today sounds louder than my struggle. I thank you, Lord. While she is shouting in heaven, I'm going to shout down here on earth. Thank you, Almighty God!

Upon the passing of my mother-in-law, I have to live in a state of praising God during the time of the struggle. She is the ultimate inspiration for a life-changing experience for me. This phenomenal life-changing experience is now something I am actually experiencing for myself instead of just witnessing others do. I have not witnessed many people who were able to praise God in the midst of a struggle. In fact, I have only had the privilege of seeing this in action with two people in my entire life: my deceased mother-in-law and my father. These two people lived and live a life in which their praise is so great that you would really have to be close to them to understand that there is or ever was a struggle apparent in their life. In fact, I can't promise that I ever viewed the two of them as people who struggled.

I would describe my dad as a very optimistic and a dynamic man of faith. I had always dismissed his faith and his optimism because of the fact that he was a minister, and that optimism was, in essence, his job. My mother-in-law could be described in a way very similar to my dad. She was always showing others the bright side of things, she had a very giving nature, so yes, she was optimistic and faithful. Not only did these two people very close to me have the same praise, they also had the same struggle. The two of them were diagnosed with cancer. My father was diagnosed with prostate cancer, and a year later, my mother-in-law was diagnosed with breast cancer. Cancer was the only struggle that I could define in their lives. However, never did either one of them profess cancer as ever being a struggle; in fact through all the treatments, radiation, and surgeries, all I could ever see was the power of praise in the both of them. The cancer was never the prevailing factor in their lives. The two of them never empowered cancer with their words and their actions. Instead, their praise rang louder than their struggle.

Chapter 1

The Plan

◇◇◇◇◇◇◇◇◇◇◇◇◇◇◇◇◇◇◇◇◇◇◇◇◇◇◇◇

"For I know the plans I have for you," declares the Lord, "plans to prosper you and not to harm you, plans to give you hope and a future."
—*Jeremiah 29:11 (NIV)*

While some days appear to be better than others, those really rough days that I struggled getting through made me question the plan that God had for me. I could not see prosperity; instead I saw harm. I could not see a plan of prosperity after being unemployed for ten months, nor hope for future that consisted of more than grieving the loss of my mother-in-law. That is not to mention the many side effects and circumstances that surrounded these two traumatic experiences of death and unemployment. Most of all, it was extremely difficult for me to find the motivation to praise God for the work that was taking place in my life. God was working His plan in my life, but this was nothing like what I ever could have imagined. I simply did not understand His plan for my life, and I began to question it. Thankfully, I had just enough of a spiritual foundation where I never question God's allowance of these occurrences; I just began to question *why me* and *why now*.

I would not say that I am a person that needs to be in control. However, I am a planner. In fact, those who know me will often hear me say that as long as I can plan for it, then I am okay. I need a heads-up; I need a warning. I can adapt to change as long as I know it's coming and can plan for the changes. I planned to have my children at ages twenty-seven and thirty, and if I had had a third one, it would have been at age thirty-three. Sometimes my planning can be seen as being very organized and prepared for every situation or event in my life. However, in the spiritual realm, this need for planning and advance knowledge can be debilitating; it's an area of my life that contradicted my spiritual belief, my faith. Faith is the exact opposite of the one thing I craved the most—knowing the plan. Faith requires that you trust and believe in what you don't see, and therefore you can't plan for what you don't know is coming. I tried very hard to reconcile and justify that it was not a lack of faith. In my heart, I had faith that God would take care of me and my family, but there was just this one important detail that I needed to know, and that was how God was going to take care of me and my family. I wanted to know God's exact plan. I needed the details of how He was going to do it, when He was going to do it, and in what manner was He was going to work His plan in my life. I came to a very humbling place and recognized that I had faith in God in theory but not in practice. I had faith that God could do the unthinkable. I had enough faith to believe that God was a miracle worker. I had faith that God would supply all of my needs, according to His riches in glory. I had faith in God, but I didn't have faith in His unseen process.

From this place in my heart is where God would begin His transformation in my life. One of the most wonderful qualities about God is His willingness to put before you the very thing that you need to see manifested in the natural. One day, as a daily devotional, I received the scripture of Jeremiah 29:11, and of course, being in the state of mind that I was in, I was hungry to receive this word. A couple of weeks later, our church had Collegiate Sunday, a Sunday service that allows our college students to lead worship service. On this particular Sunday, the emphasized scripture was taken from, you guessed it, Jeremiah 29:11, which says: "For I know the plans I have for you declares the Lord, plans to prosper you, and not to harm you, plans to give you hope and a future." This scripture text would help me acknowledge that I needed to increase my faith in order to arrive at a new level and dimension of his manifestation of power and glory.

God has a plan for me. It's a plan that I will prosper and not be harmed, and it is a plan that gives me hope and a future. The more I said this scripture, the more I began to see the very power of this scripture. The scripture of Jeremiah 29:11 is often quoted in partiality. For example, I always hear others say God has plan for me. I also hear people say I don't know what the future holds for me, but God knows. There is another reference to this scripture when people of the faith say, "I will trust in the will of the Lord." It is important that we really look at every word and meaning of this powerful scripture. The beginning of the scripture says: "For I know the plans I have for you; declares the Lord." The Lord declared this to us, meaning that He wanted to formally, loudly, and boldly announce this truth that He knows the plans that He has for His people. Notice that God did not say *plan*—in the singular. God said *plans* in the plural. This is important because we often categorize our lives as one big situation or event; whereas God looks at every intricate detail and moment of our life. The scripture acknowledges that He has an answer for every single struggle, event, action, and moment that happens in our lives. He tells us boldly and emphatically that He knows all about the events and struggles. I began to realize that I, like others who relied on their own plans, was shocked, caught off guard, and emotionally driven by these events in my life. In particular for me, I was shocked because my faith was limited. Remember, I needed to know that it was all going to happen; instead, I just came into the knowledge of them. However, God is not threatened, shaken, or dismayed at these events because He knew that they were going to take place.

The revelation of this knowledge that God is not dismayed or shocked by these occurrences is plainly stated in the second part of this scripture which states that these plans, which I define as answers to these events and struggles in my life, are plans that He has that will lead us to prosperity, hope, and a future. I point out here the syntax of the words "hope *and a* future" versus how it is often quoted as "hope *for* a future." These two conjunctions make a big difference; hope for a future implies that you may not have a future but it looks promising; while hope and a future gives us both hope and a future. God's plans for his people leads them to greatness and prosperity.

My faith began to increase gradually, and I began to receive the words in the scripture that God has plans for me that lead me to happiness. However, I was still not at the point of understanding that His plans involve struggle. I want to be very clear; I knew that in this life I would have trials and tribulations, but before that time in my life, the trials and tribulations were all mingled together with being a saved and sanctified Christian. In other words, I just accepted the struggles. I recognized that I was limiting the unleashing of God's power. Contrary to that form of passive responsiveness, I went a small step further and recognized that God's plan is the answer to struggle—God's plan is *not* the struggle.

Remember, God does know that the struggles are going to take place in your life and in His plan; His answer for the struggle is what should be our focus. God allows struggles that we often define as trials and tribulations. God knows, and scriptures tell us, that evil is ever present and that the enemy comes to steal, kill, and destroy. We can quote this all day long, but we fail to stand on the fact that God has the plans—the answers—to these trials. The perfect example of this in the Bible is the story of Job. Every time that I have heard the story of Job told, the emphasis was on the struggles that took place. Job lost everything he had; flesh fell from his bones, and God allowed it happen. Our flesh allows us to often sympathize with Job and waddle in the misery of depression and oppression. However, if we would get to the end and the true meaning of the story of Job, we could then see the praise and the plans of God at work.

Satan believed that the only reason why Job continued to praise and worship God is because God had, in essence, blessed him with so many material things. Satan often would have us to look at the outside and tangible things in our life as a way of marking our relationship with God instead of marking our relationship with God and His connection with us by what is deep in our hearts. I have categorized this view of prosperity as *physical prosperity versus spiritual prosperity*. Satan was looking and acknowledging all of the physical prosperity of Job. We are attracted to Job's physical strength, large cattle, family unit, large homes, and several acres of land. God, however, was looking at his spiritual prosperity, as seen in Job's faithfulness, dedication to the ministry, and his continuous praise to God. Satan believes that God bribes his people to praise and worship him by giving them material items. The only reason why Job was praising God, according to Satan, was because he had everything a man could ever want and need.

Another increase in my faith and self-awareness, while hard for me to admit and come to terms with because I, too, felt guilty and lived out this concept of the belief of Satan, came when I realized I only praised God for the material prosperity. The only difference between myself and Satan was that I didn't think that God gave me these things as a bribe for me to praise Him, but I most certainly didn't behave any differently. I wasn't really in a place where I was offering up praises to God. I was more in a place where I was begging and pleading with God. I knew that I had blessings that I didn't deserve and that I was not as perfect as Job. I felt that I could relate to Job and could testify that I, too, was physically prosperous. However, Job and I differed in our levels of spiritual prosperity. The scriptures have already proven that we can't tempt the Lord our God, and therefore Satan can't really dare God to do anything. Satan's dare to God is not why God responded; instead the plan that God had for Job through this story is to demonstrate two things: God's Word never fails, and He will bless those who earnestly seek Him and praise Him. God's plan for Job was to allow Satan to take away all Job's physical prosperity, including his health and his family, only so that God could show His power.

I found comfort in relating to Job's struggle during this period of my life. I remember quoting phrases to myself such as, "If Job waited on the Lord, why can't I?" I was just relating Job's struggles to mine, but I never looked past the struggles to see God's plans for Job's life nor my own life. I waddled in the story of Job because I was unemployed, grieving a significant loss, and could not see any means of a prosperous future. Thankfully, the other commonality that I had with Job was that while we both cursed the day and absolutely hated what we were going through, we never cursed God. God knew that Job would not curse Him, and He knew that I would not curse Him either. Thus, God once again showed me and Job and all who experience struggles that His Word stands and will never fail. This is good news because if we believe and stand on this scripture alone, then we will recognize that God will give us a life filled with prosperity.

God returned back to Job seven times the amount of physical possessions Job lost because Job never ceased to praise him. Those who acquire spiritual prosperity first will see the manifestation of physical prosperity in greater depths than what man could ever offer. I was eventually able to develop and gain a clearer understanding of this concept and story. The story of Job helped increase my faith in God's power and plan and not my plan and my struggles. But, I must admit I was still at a point where I posed these questions: *Why me and Job, Lord? Why now and what for?* Still very much in a physical and selfish mindset, I wanted to really know why God chose my and Job's life to manifest this power.

Remember that God has the plans—the answers—and nothing that is taking place is shocking to Him because He knows these things are going to happen. In the case of Job, it was not about him; it was about the witness that God was going to use to show others. The story of Job is told to the believers as well as to the unbelievers. The story is so powerful that those who don't read the Bible or don't believe in it tell the story to this day in the form of a fable. Either way, the power of God is revealed and all who respect the story enough continue to apply the story to their daily lives. I began to see that I should count it an honor to be used by God to show his power and to give strength to others. The struggle that you may be going through doesn't mean that you have done something wrong, that you have been disobedient, or that God is testing you. Your perceived struggle sometimes is God's plan, His answer to an attack that Satan is designed for you or someone else. Our purpose is to draw all men to Him. How can we draw others if we can't model for them the true power of Christ? My faith is increased through the story of Job because Job helped me realize that God's plan involves me having spiritual prosperity and physical prosperity. The story of Job is one that demonstrated the power of praising God for the victory that He has already declared and spoken over our lives.

Another Bible story that helped me deal with why God allowed these sufferings in my life during this time (and many more times to come) is the story about the blind man. In my opinion, it is one of the most interesting stories in the New Testament. I find the blind man to be a dynamic person. This is a man who was born blind, yet he brings the light of Jesus to those of us who think they can see. The story of the blind man showed me Christ's response toward what I describe as undeserved suffering. My suffering seemed undeserved. I worked hard for everything I had, I tried to serve the Lord with all my heart. I prayed and was diligent to do the will of the Lord; at least in my mind I was doing all of those things. I was at that point of asking that infamous question: Why me, Lord? I would imagine that at some point in all of our spiritual walks, we ask that same or similar question: Why me, Lord? Why was I born blind, born poor, born with this affliction, why did I have to suffer the abuse of domestic violence, cancer, the sudden death of a loved one, job loss, chronic illness, a low IQ, prison, wayward children, and on and on so that we could ask the "Why me, Lord?" question. And this story about the blind man is where I see Jesus giving me the answer to the question to why these struggles are taking place in my life.

We are not given much information about the blind man. We don't even know his name. We know that he lived in darkness his entire life. He was known in the city as a beggar, and the only support he received was from the generosity of others around him. Given his condition, I don't think the man ever thought he would be healed or thought it even possible to see again. Two very important events take place with the blind man. First, notice how the blind man didn't approach Jesus. Nobody ever brought him to Jesus, nor had he ever asked to be healed. Yet, two things happened to him in the course of this chapter. He was healed physically, and then, after going through an incredible gauntlet of challenges, he was healed spiritually as well.

When the blind man encountered Jesus, scripture indicates that Jesus was escaping from the Pharisees and other Jewish leaders. Jesus was in somewhat of a major dispute with them because he had professed to be the son of God—one with the Father. They accused Jesus of blasphemy and ran to find stones that they would use to stone Jesus to death. Therefore, the scriptures said, Jesus hid himself, going through the midst of them, and he slipped away in the crowd. As Jesus is escaping and going out through the temple gate, we are introduced to the blind man, and it was in this context that Jesus approached the blind man. The blind man often sat by one of the exits of the Jewish temple, which would make sense as he would probably beg for money as the people walked in and out. Can't you see our thoughts playing out in scripture as this story unfolds? Many of us think that God is too busy, He doesn't see us, and He can't feel us suffering, so we try to manipulate Him to work and move on our time.

The devil tricks us by engaging our minds in dialogues that are man-centered instead of Jesus-centered. We have thoughts, such as I need to network with the right people, and we buy into sayings, such as "It's not what you know; it's who you know." We often think that we need to look a certain kind of way to get the attention of the room, or we need to talk a certain way to get to the position. But, I love the fact that Jesus found this man in his worst spot, in his begging position. Jesus stops for him when the blind man is at his worst and lowest point. Jesus reminded me that in my worst spot, the best place that I could be to see Jesus is where the blind man was: in church. So, no matter how low I get, no matter how rough it seems, in my worst and best place in life, the church is where I need to be positioned.

Take notice at what happened when Jesus approached the blind man. He didn't engage him in prolonged discussion. He did not ask him questions. He did not tell the man to follow him and become his disciple. He did not discuss the man's past or his sins. He didn't tell him, like he told Nicodemus, that he had to be born again. No, Jesus immediately went to work. "He spit on the ground, made some mud with the saliva, and put it on the man's eyes" (John 9:6). Jesus didn't stop there; he then gave the blind man an assignment. "Go," he told him, "wash in the pool of Siloam." So the man went and washed, and came home seeing" (John 9:7). I wondered if the blind man even questioned or thought about what Jesus was telling him to do. Did he think it was strange; did he think that this would not work? I found it fascinating that he just did it. Sometimes God allows us to get to that point of lowliness so that we don't interfere with His method and His plan. When you get a word from God, it will not be like any other word you have received or heard. You will move, and you will be ready to do exactly what He tells you to do.

I love the way Jesus moved on without ever waiting to see the man's outcome. The blind man and Jesus would meet again later on, and when they did, the blind man immediately began to worship Jesus. The blind man became a true disciple, a witness that Jesus had healed Him. This is the only recorded instance in the whole Bible where a person who was born blind was healed by the power of God. The disciples couldn't bear to let this opportunity slip away. They were just like you and I would have been. All their lives, they had wondered about this age-old problem of pain. If God is a good God and all powerful, why on earth would God allow a person to be struck down with such a problem? It was easy enough to understand if this person had been some despicable person; he would deserve to be punished. But this poor fellow was totally blind from the very beginning of his life. When he came out of the womb, he couldn't see. He had lived in total darkness. And so the disciples raised this question to their teacher: "Rabbi, who sinned, this man or his parents, that he was born blind?" I didn't ask the question in this way, but it came from the same place in my heart—*Lord, what did I do or someone in my life do for me to deserve these struggles and this pain?*

How did Jesus respond? Did he respond like we sometimes do as parents when our children question us? "Because I said so." It is a question that I want answered from the place of child, such as why is the sky blue, and if anyone can give me the answer, it should be the Son of God. I am waiting to hear the answer to why we have trials and struggles from the one who can solve all of my problems. His answer is not complex, it is not filled with lengthy explanations, and he doesn't even have to go into a long sermon to give the answer. Instead Jesus said, "but that the works of God should be made manifest in him. I must work the works of him that sent me, while it is day: the night cometh, when no man can work.

The Plan

As long as I am in the world, I am the light of the world" (John 9:4–5). The same response that Jesus gave is still His response to you and me today. Instead of asking Jesus why did this happen to you or others, start responding to His will in your life. I changed my prayer to be more like asking God to show me how His work is going to be manifested in my life? I stopped questioning and I began praising.

God wants to do a mighty work in your life, right in the place of your brokenness, right at the spot that you are in. It will be a work so great that others in the natural world will not be able to identify you and will not believe that you are the same person. Later on in the scripture, we see the people who once knew him as the blind begging man see him come back as the vibrant man with vision, telling about a man named Jesus who found him, touched him, and healed his body. At least three times in the passage, we read about people questioning if it was really him, questioning the miracle of Jesus, and questioning the process.

This time, it's the reply of the blind man that gives me strength. "Yes, I am the blessed one." The blind man had one encounter with Jesus, and he was totally reformed and changed. The blind man showed me that all it takes is one encounter with the Lord, and my circumstances can totally change. The change will be so sudden and transformative that people may not even be able to recognize you or offer an explanation. Once your breakthrough comes, once your healing comes, once your promotion comes, whatever your barrier may be, you too will be able to look at the nonbeliever, the doubters, and testify just like the blind man and say "I am the blessed one. I have had an encounter with God. God has used me to manifest his power and his glory in my life."

It will not be long when people will be asking the same questions that the blind man's neighbors were asking about you, and you will respond like the blind man:

- How can it be that you didn't have the education, but you got the job? I am the blessed one.
- How can it be that you were just borrowing money, but now you are lending the money? I am the blessed one.
- How can it be that you were beaten, molested, and abused, but you still can love again? I am the blessed one.
- How can it be that when we talked about you, your family and that your kids were not acting right, and were in and out of jail, that you didn't lose your mind? I am the blessed one.

I feel my praise rising up from within and getting louder and louder as I realize that God has a plan. I know that God has a plan for my life, and I don't have to know the details of the plan, which is enough to make me want to give him praise. Therefore, it's time for a *praise break!*

Praise Break

Prayer: Father God, I thank you for speaking to me through your Word. Lord, I ask that you let that same word you put before me several times be put into the hearts of every reader: "For I know the plans I have for you," declares the Lord, "plans to prosper you and not to harm you, plans to give you hope and a future." God, I recognize that it is in my struggle that you will manifest your power. Father, I change my prayer from *Why me, Lord?* to *Thank you, Lord, for choosing to manifest your miracles in my life.* God, I ask that you open my eyes and heal my spiritual blindness; let me see your plan. Lord, let me move forward with your plan like the blind man, never questioning your process.

The Plan

Scriptures:

John 16:33:
These things I have spoken to you, so that in Me you may have peace. In the world you have tribulation, but take courage; I have overcome the world.

Philippians 1:6 (NIV):
…being confident of this, that he who began a good work in you will carry it on to completion until the day of Christ Jesus.

Romans 15:13 (NIV):
May the God of hope fill you with all joy and peace as you trust in him, so that you may overflow with hope by the power of the Holy Spirit.

Proverbs 3:5-6:
Trust in the Lord with all thine heart; and lean not unto thine own understanding.
In all thy ways acknowledge him, and he shall direct thy paths.

Proverbs 16:1-4 (NIV):
To humans belong the plans of the heart, but from the Lord comes the proper answer of the tongue. All a person's ways seem pure to them, but motives are weighed by the Lord. Commit to the Lord whatever you do, and he will establish your plans. The Lord works out everything to its proper end—even the wicked for a day of disaster.

2 Corinthians 4:17-18 (NIV):
For our light and momentary troubles are achieving for us an eternal glory that far outweighs them all. So we fix our eyes not on what

is seen, but on what is unseen, since what is seen is temporary, but what is unseen is eternal.

Lamentations 3:21-23 (NIV):
Yet this I call to mind and therefore I have hope: Because of the Lord's great love we are not consumed, for his compassions never fail. They are new every morning; great is your faithfulness.

Chapter 2
The Growth Mindset

◇◇◇◇◇◇◇◇◇◇◇◇◇◇◇◇◇◇◇◇◇◇◇◇◇◇◇◇

Finally, brethren, whatsoever things are true, whatsoever things are honest, whatsoever things are just, whatsoever things are pure, whatsoever things are lovely, whatsoever things are of good report; if there be any virtue, and if there be any praise, think on these things.

—*Philippians 4:8*

One of the greatest attacks that the devil used on me was the feeling of hopelessness. He wanted me to think that I had no options. He came in my thoughts and knew that if he attacked my emotions, he could stop me from growing. I needed to move from a fixed mindset to a growth mindset. My mind was fixed and set on the struggle. I had to get my mind right. There was little room for me to see where growth could come out of this desolate place. After all, a bank account cannot grow without a paycheck coming in every month, or could it?

Well, when I changed my mindset from a fixed mindset to a growth mindset, I started to realize that my bank account could grow without a paycheck coming in every month. A fixed mindset believes that money only comes from the payroll department of an employer. However, a growth mindset believes that God can dispatch money from any source He chooses, and therefore, He *is* the employer. A fixed mindset traps one into their current situation and denies them of hope for anything different. A fixed mindset puts limitations on how God can manifest in our lives, while a growth mindset breeds God's favor, blessings, and miracles. If the devil could get me to fix my mind on the situation, then he knew that I would not get to the blessings, the true outpouring of God's abundance and the love that He wanted to demonstrate in my life.

I must admit, it is hard to see the blessings of God when you are struggling. Negative thoughts and actions are all around you, and these feelings are very real. A fixed mindset doesn't mean that you negate the raw emotions that you experience. This is not about ignoring or suppressing that you are depressed, sad, and hurting. However, the growth mindset is about understanding that even in the midst of all of this pain, God is still ever present. Therefore, I rested, assured that I would not be in this place forever. I often heard other believers say that we are in spiritual warfare. There was a war going on, and it was in my mind; it's a spiritual warfare. The world would have me to think that I was in a physical battle, and the physical warfare is playing out right in front of my eyes, but those wars start in the mind.

The enemy begins by placing these negative thoughts in your mind and spirit. As a mother, educator, wife, and sister, I constantly feel the attacks of the enemy. I started to realize that the enemy wanted me to feel defeated and unhappy. How does Satan do this? He would sneak in through conversations, media outlets, and small encounters that amounted to big events in my mind. In particular, I often would compare myself to others. Until I became aware of what I was doing, I would not think that I was comparing myself. Instead I would say that, "I am just benchmarking." Slowly and bit by bit, piece by piece, those innocent benchmarks would turn into tiny scratches, scrapes, cuts, burns, and bruises.

It is important to note that I didn't get to this place overnight. There were innocent influencers and influences of the past that shaped my outlook. Upon my reflection, I realized that what started as a very pleasant and rewarding experience in my life was now affecting me negatively. For example, I used to compete in pageant competitions. The pageants that I would enter would award the winner with the title of queen, of course, but I would also get scholarship money for college. In fact, several times my winnings supplemented my college expenses. I gained a lot of skills by competing in pageants, such as interviewing, honing my vocal performance talent, public speaking, and communicating within diverse environments. The same way all of those positive skills and talents that I gained became a part of my natural character, so was competing.

Competing was now embedded in my spirit. I competed without realizing it; it became as natural as walking. You don't have teammates in pageants; it's just you competing against the other young ladies. My critiques were not about another teammate, the coach, the play call, and so forth. My critiques were directly about my talent, my interview, my poise, or lack thereof. Now life became a competition for me, and I was constantly on the stage. Therefore, if I am not "winning," then it is because I lacked the skills necessary and was not prepared enough in that endeavor to win.

The problem is, now I am in the competition of life, and it didn't seem like I even had the requirements to sign up. How do I compete with cancer, how do I compete with death, how do I compete with a job loss, how do I compete with what I have been given and be the trophy wife, perfect mother, and game changer? I did not feel like I was winning at all. I had placed myself in this artificial competition, and worse yet, I was losing and feeling very defeated.

It was important that I begin to recognize that these attacks were influencing my mood and my emotions. The devil had every intention for me to stay in a place where God was not able to move about freely. Satan wanted me to stay fixed in a place of unrest, a place of non-growth. It became hard to separate the will of God from when I allowed Satan's attack. Therefore, it became hard for me to praise God, worship freely, and have joy. I was fixed on believing that God just wanted me to go through these trials and stay in this place.

But fortunately, through the reading of the words of Paul, I was reminded that God actually wanted me to have joy. In fact, the entire book of Philippians is actually all about how to have joy and a peace that surpasses all understanding. I am still struggling, I am still in a war, but God is saying I should have joy. This paradoxical thinking that I can have a peaceful war and therefore a joyful struggle was hard for me imagine, let alone live out. Therefore, the question became: how do I have peace of mind in the midst of war? The answer was always in front of me, but I couldn't see it, or I guess I should say it was easier said than done.

> *"Finally, brethren, whatsoever things are true, whatsoever things are honest, whatsoever things are just, whatsoever things are pure, whatsoever things are lovely, whatsoever things are of good report; if there be any virtue, and if there be any praise, think on these things."* —Phil. 4:8

The answer was apparent: whatever I put in my mind is what would come out.

Okay, God, so you are telling me if I put the right things into my mind, the right things will come out? I have also heard it stated in this manner: What the mind attends to, it considers; what the mind does not attend to, it dismisses; what the mind attends to continually, it believes; and what the mind believes, it does. It starts with what we are putting into our minds. I liken it to the hydrologic cycle (the water cycle). If we were to replace the water with our thoughts in the water cycle, look at the cycle we would create.

Evaporation: The transfer of water from the surface of the Earth to the atmosphere. The main factors affecting evaporation are temperature, humidity, wind speed, and solar radiation. The principal source of water vapor comes from oceans, but evaporation also occurs in soil, snow, and ice.[1]

Spiritual Evaporation: The transfer of thoughts from the surface of the heart to the atmosphere. The main factors affecting spiritual evaporation are faith, impartations, timing, and nurturing. The principal source of thoughts comes from hearing and receiving the Word of God; this could be through the form of reading, teaching, preaching, singing, and meditating.

Condensation: Condensation will take place as soon as the air contains more water vapor than it can receive from a free water surface through evaporation at the prevailing temperature. This condition occurs as the consequence of either cooling or the mixing of air masses of different temperatures. By condensation, water vapor is released to form precipitation.[2]

Spiritual Condensation: Spiritual condensation will take place as soon as the heart and mind contain more spiritual thoughts than negative thoughts received and believed from any of the prevailing emotions of the human spirit through a sort of spiritual evaporation. This condition occurs as the consequence of either accepting or denying the Word of the Lord. By spiritual condensation, our thoughts are released to form a precipitation of emotions, thoughts, and ideas.

Precipitation: Precipitation that falls to the earth is distributed in four main ways: some returns to the atmosphere by evaporation, some is intercepted by vegetation and then evaporated from the surface of leaves, some percolates into the soil by infiltration, and the remainder flows directly as surface runoff into the sea.[3]

Spiritual Precipitation: Spiritual precipitation that falls from our minds is distributed in four main ways: some returns back to our minds because we are fearful to let it go, some may be intercepted by those that are around us and then evaporated from their actions, some percolates into the hearts and souls of those around us, and the remainder flows directly as surface runoff into the lives of those under our influence.

Our thoughts flow in the same manner of the water cycle. The water from the earth evaporates and condenses into the clouds, the clouds fill up, and once filled, then cause precipitation, and this water falls back to the earth, starting the cycle again. One of my classroom posters state: "Watch your thoughts; they become your words. Watch your words; they become your actions. Watch your actions; they become your character." Just as water cycles, so do our thoughts, and our thoughts become our character for good or bad. In the water cycle, the water comes from the different sources of the earth. It is important that you recognize the source of where your thoughts come from. If you are constantly repeating the cycle of negative, hopeless, defeated thoughts, then that is what you are going to produce. Paul was keenly aware that people of God needed to first have the knowledge of who God has called us to be and who we are in Christ. Paul knew that whatever knowledge he poured into them, they would in turn pour out to others. Paul tells us that there are three main ways to get our minds right, and that is to think carefully, righteously, and actively.

Think Carefully

The Bible commands us to think deeply to mediate for a period of time on the scriptures. The problem becomes that we are not meditating on the things of Christ, instead of thinking carefully, we are thinking recklessly. We allow our minds to drift to the situation and not the promises, on the worries of yesterday and not the gift of today. Once we begin to ponder on all the wrong that we have done and not the mercy that God has shown, then we have begun to meditate and ponder on reckless thoughts. Thinking is critical. "As a man thinketh, so is he." We will walk out our thoughts; we will wear our thoughts in action. The Bible commands us to think: "Come now, let us reason together" (Isa. 1:18). In other words, instead of just yielding to circumstances, think about how God has and will deliver. Think about Jesus! Jesus said "Learn of Me," and we know that "My people perish because of the lack of knowledge." If you are not thinking correctly, you will surely die. We need to think, we need to think carefully, and we need to think righteously.

Think Righteously

> I find it important to note what neuroscientists and experts have all reported about our thoughts. *"Experts estimate that the mind thinks between 60,000—80,000 thoughts a day. That's an average of 2,500-3,300 thoughts per hour. That's incredible. Other experts estimate a smaller number, of 50,000 thoughts per day, which means about 2,100 thoughts per hour. Of those, 80% are negative and 95% are exactly the same repetitive thoughts as the day before."*[4]

If we were to go by what we believe is occurring each day with our minds, the research would suggest that the average person is repeating negative thoughts over and over each day. Therefore, the Bible makes it clear that we have to change the source of thoughts and meditate/think on the things that are righteous. If we think righteously, we will think as Paul tells us to: "Finally, brethren, whatsoever things are true, whatsoever things are honest, whatsoever things are just, whatsoever things are pure, whatsoever things are lovely, whatsoever things are of good report; if there be any virtue, and if there be any praise, think on these things" (Phil. 4:8). Righteous thinking creates a new thought cycle because true things are noble, noble things are honest, honest things are just, just things are pure, pure things are lovely, and lovely things, therefore, lead us to praise.

It can be hard to discern what the truth is today. Well, fortunately, our God specializes in truth. He said "My Word is true, and it will last." You have to discern what is right and what is wrong; there simply are no alternative facts. Alternative facts, if not scripture, are false statements and teachings. Another popular saying that we are allowing to stand up as truth is "I am speaking *my* truth," and we are even encouraged to "speak your truth" and yes, you should be true about whether you are in the will of God or not, but if your truth is not aligned to the Word of God, then you are standing on false sanctity. Realize that we all fall short of the glory of God through our sins; we should seek repentance and focus on the fact that Jesus died so that we may be free and forgiven—that is the truth.

Think Actively

If we want to start a new habit, we have to do it repetitively. I happen to be a hands-on learner—I learn by doing. I have heard people say once I actually drive to a new place, I don't have to look at the directions to get back home, but if I didn't drive to it, then I need to use the directions. It is the same requirement for thinking. You have to actively engage in your meditative practices. You can't separate the thought life from what you practice. If you begin to accept the Word of God as true, then you will actively live out the Word of God. If you put the Word of God inside of you and think and mediate on the scriptures, then you will produce the fruits of the spirit.

Praise Break

Prayer: Lord, I thank you for giving me a mindset of growth. I praise you because today I recognize that I don't have to stay in the place that I am in, that growth is still taking place in my life. Give me strength and courage to act out my belief in you by offering to you the highest praise that I can give you in the midst of every circumstance. Show me the distractions and negative influences of everything that is keeping my mind from meditating on your Word. Lord, give me discernment and revelation knowledge to help me see the truth in every situation.

Scriptures:

3 John 1:2
Beloved, I wish about all things that thou mayest prosper and be in health, even as thy soul prospereth.

Psalm 103 (NIV)
>*1 Praise the LORD, my soul; all my inmost being, praise his holy name.*
>*2 Praise the LORD, my soul, and forget not all his benefits—*
>*3 who forgives all your sins and heals all your diseases,*
>*4 who redeems your life from the pit and crowns you with love and compassion,*
>*5 who satisfies your desires with good things so that your youth is renewed like the eagle's.*
>*6 The LORD works righteousness and justice for all the oppressed.*
>*7 He made known his ways to Moses, his deeds to the people of Israel:*
>*8 The LORD is compassionate and gracious, slow to anger, abounding in love.*

9 He will not always accuse, nor will he harbor his anger forever;
10 he does not treat us as our sins deserve or repay us according to our iniquities.
11 For as high as the heavens are above the earth, so great is his love for those who fear him;
12 as far as the east is from the west, so far has he removed our transgressions from us.
13 As a father has compassion on his children, so the LORD has compassion on those who fear him;
14 for he knows how we are formed, he remembers that we are dust.
15 The life of mortals is like grass, they flourish like a flower of the field;
16 the wind blows over it and it is gone, and its place remembers it no more.
17 But from everlasting to everlasting the LORD's love is with those who fear him, and his righteousness with their children's children
18 with those who keep his covenant and remember to obey his precepts.
19 The LORD has established his throne in heaven, and his kingdom rules over all.
20 Praise the LORD, you his angels, you mighty ones who do his bidding, who obey his word.
21 Praise the LORD, all his heavenly hosts, you his servants who do his will.
22 Praise the LORD, all his works everywhere in his dominion. Praise the LORD, my soul.

Chapter 3

The Divine Delivery

◇◇◇◇◇◇◇◇◇◇◇◇◇◇◇◇◇◇◇◇◇◇◇◇◇

"But about midnight Paul and Silas were praying and singing hymns of praise to God, and the prisoners were listening to them; and suddenly there came a great earthquake, so that the foundations of the prison house were shaken; and immediately all the doors were opened and everyone's chains were unfastened."

—Acts 16:25-26

I constantly had to revisit the concept that God's plan was the answer to my struggles. His plan for my life and my perceived struggles still lived very close in my thoughts. I was still asking God to bless me instead of praising Him for His plan. One of the reasons that I think this was difficult for me and for others is that sometimes God's plan appears to be a struggle. In the story of Paul and Silas, God's plan was for the two men to be imprisoned; prison appears to be a struggle. God's plan was also to send an earthquake; an earthquake appears to be a struggle. It is not until the entire plan was revealed that we are able to see the miraculous power of God's plan. Our entire purpose in life is to deliver others and bring more souls to Jesus. In order to live in this world, we must be delivered. We are constantly vacillating between being delivered and being the deliverer; and when God is really moving in one's life; they will find themselves in both places, just as Paul and Silas. God has the ultimate plan, and His plan is always about deliverance. When God is in charge of the delivery, I call it a divine delivery. You can recognize a divine delivery once you have experienced one, but until you come into the knowledge and obtain this faith in God, this delivery will appear to be a struggle.

God sent the earthquake when Paul and Silas were chained in jail. I am certain that everyone else around struggled to find the goodness in this earthquake. However, the plan of God was to perform a divine delivery, and therefore, when the earth shook, the chains were unfastened and the doors of the prison opened. Paul and Silas became free because of a divine delivery. God's plan was not just to prove that he could deliver Paul and Silas out of prison. It was more than just a simple delivery; our God is complex. Remember, while you are being delivered, you can be delivering others simultaneously. As the story of Paul and Silas continues, we recognize their true work in prison. Once the security guard woke up, he realized that all of the prisoners had been set free. This caused the security guard to turn the sword on himself and attempt to commit suicide—until Paul and Silas spoke to him. This moment was when they began to see the purpose for having been put in prison. They began to speak to the security guard and minister to him the words of salvation. The world thought that they had placed Paul and Silas in prison, but it was truly God who planned for them to go to prison.

I think about many other religious leaders whom man thought they placed in prison. Leaders such as Martin Luther King, Jr. and Gandhi were placed in prison, and just like Paul and Silas, they were viewed as struggling leaders, and the emphasis was placed on them being in prison. I would like to take a moment to place the emphasis of the ministry that both of these men delivered while waiting on their delivery. Martin Luther King, wrote the sermon "Loving your Enemies" while in jail for committing nonviolent civil disobedience during the Montgomery boycott. He also wrote a letter from the Birmingham jail that was so powerful that it became a manifesto for the civil rights revolution and placed Martin Luther King among America's most renowned essayists. He was compared with Henry David Thoreau and Ralph Waldo Emerson. I found this letter to be pivotal because he was addressing this letter to local clergyman in Birmingham, Alabama who were criticizing him for coming to their city and creating what seemed to be confusion and uproar that King brought to their city. The leaders focused on the struggles and the imprisonment only. These leaders were wrapped up in the emotions of the moment and did not recognize the Spirit of the Lord at work. Leading and responding with your emotions can be dangerous.

Definition of Emotions

- Emotions: A natural instinctive state of mind deriving from one's circumstances, mood, or relationships with others. Feeling, sentiment, sensation.
- Emotions: instinctive feeling as distinguished from reasoning or knowledge, gut feeling, instinct, intuition.[5]

Emotions are too dependent upon the circumstances and conditions going on around you, and this is can sometimes be a direct contradiction to what God is actually doing for you. Your emotions are just distractions to keep you focused on the struggle; meanwhile, God has a plan to deliver you in the midst of the unbelievers. God's plan always goes back to manifesting HHHHIS power in your life. The reality is, as Christians, God is always delivering us, saving us from the hands of the enemy. Sometimes life feels like a rollercoaster ride with the highs and lows and twist and turns; and if you are not careful, your emotions will be all over the place. But remember, God is a deliverer! So, we can be calm and rest in the assurance that God is in control and will deliver us out of every situation. If you are like me, it's not about your belief that God will deliver but is more about *when* God is going to deliver me. How long, Lord, must I continue to go through ____? How long will it take before I stop crying? How long must I stay in the wilderness?

God's Timing

> *To everything there is a season, and a time to every purpose under the heaven:*
>
> *A time to be born, and a time to die; a time to plant, and a time to pluck up that which is planted;*
>
> *A time to kill, and a time to heal; a time to break down, and a time to build up;*
>
> *A time to weep, and a time to laugh; a time to mourn, and a time to dance;*
>
> *A time to cast away stones, and a time to gather stones together; a time to embrace, and a time to refrain from embracing;*
>
> *A time to get, and a time to lose; a time to keep, and a time to cast away;*
>
> *A time to rend, and a time to sew; a time to keep silence, and a time to speak;*
>
> *A time to love, and a time to hate; a time of war, and a time of peace."*
>
> —*Ecclesiastes 3:1-8 (KJV)*

I can hear the Lord saying to me through the reading of these words that it will happen in God's time. It is very hard during the process of struggle to understand why God allows us to stay in places of pain for long periods of time. However, these periods of time are causing us to grow and develop. It is very rare to have something earlier than the time it's supposed to come to you—thus the saying "timing is everything." You have probably heard this phrase many times. There is a great deal of truth in that statement. The difference between a good joke and a bad one is a person's sense of timing.

Timing is essential when dealing with people. You don't ask for a raise when business is not going well or when the economy is down. Timing is important in cooking. The juicy hamburger on the grill is raw meat if is cooked for too little time and a clump of charcoal if it is cooked too long. Timing is important in medicine. If you catch a problem early, you will be able to treat it more effectively. Your timing is important in taking medication. If you take your medicine as directed, it will be helpful. If you skip doses, it loses its effectiveness. If you take extra doses, it can be deadly.

Timing is important in finance. When you invest in a particular stock and when you sell the particular stock will make the difference between whether you make money or lose it. Knowing when to borrow and when not to borrow is the key to financial independence. Timing is important in your spiritual life as well. It is critical to live your life with an acute awareness of God's timing for your life.

Often we think in the terms of God's timing for when I should get the victory or the outcome that I am looking for, but God's timing includes the process it takes to the victory to get to the glory. Solomon tells us that "There is an appointed time for everything. And there is a time for every event under heaven" that includes the good and the bad that life brings our way. The key word in the Ecclesiastes 3 passage is the word *time* that is used thirty times in the first eight verses. The difference with how Solomon references the events is that he doesn't call either of them good or bad; he doesn't make any judgments about the occurrences. Instead, he just records them as the natural parts of the circle of life. In other words, things will take place here on earth, so how will you respond to them? Our response varies depending on our faith and belief that God uses every one of these moments to get us to our destiny. Solomon also use the word *appointed*. Appointments don't happen by chance; they are not random acts. Anything that is appointed is intentional and has a purpose behind it. The events of our lives do not randomly happen; God has a purpose behind them. He has purpose even behind the events that seem to be the work of Satan.

We had just moved into our newly constructed home and had probably been in the home for about thirty days. One Wednesday night after coming home from church, my husband, Fernando and I were standing in the kitchen, and all of a sudden, he heard an overflow of water coming from our main floor bathroom. He immediately left the kitchen and went toward the bathroom to see what was going on. He returned to the kitchen and with a very disgusted look said to me, "Tiffany, this is bad." Moving forward the next morning, we had about thirty service vehicles, restoration services, builders, and all kinds of contractors at our home to take care of this problem. There was no denying that there was problem, but all of these people were interested in knowing who was responsible for the problem. Fernando and I just wanted the problem to be fixed. Due to the placement of the pipe that was flowing to this bathroom, the workers had to dig into the concrete of our porch and sidewalk just to access the problem. Then, due to the flooding, they had to take up some hardwood flooring, cut open some sheetrock, and pull up the carpet and tile in all the affected areas. Our new home was in shambles. We had just gone from walking through perfection to being back at a place of construction.

We were in contact with the head of every division of the project; everyone wanted to see who was at fault because that determined who was going to pay for the damages. Everyone who came to our home was so surprised by my reaction. I think I was even surprised by my reaction. Literally, I quote one of the representatives from the builder, "Most people would have a gun to our heads and cursing us out with not-so-pretty words." Yet, in the midst of all of this, I was in a happy place. I began to understand Solomon in this passage; even though this looked like a very bad experience, because of the timing, it was good for this to occur because it happened under the warranty period. Under warranty meant our family did not have to incur any monetary cost to take care of the problem. It also increased the sense of urgency for the builders; they would not let this problem stay as paperwork on the desk, so we were the active priority. Another reason I was happy was because God had timed Fernando's and my arrival to the kitchen to be just in time so that we could hear the water and catch the problem quickly. Because we did, the damage was not as exhaustive as it could have been, and we were free from worries about mold and mildew.

I began to think about how discouraged I was when I ordered my furniture, and they told me that my order would not be delivered until the following month. I smiled again and realized that God knew that this would happen—the area where there was damage had no furniture in it at that time and therefore could not be damaged. I have come to realize that God's ways are not our ways and his thoughts are not our thoughts. God's plan is greater than anything we could ever imagine. Solomon reminded me that we serve a God who appoints both our birthday and the day of our funeral. There are absolutely no surprises with God. He is so sovereign that there is nothing or anybody who stop his divine appointments and timing for our lives.

Embracing the Season

I am beginning to embrace whatever season of life that I am in, knowing that it's the season that I need for the God's great plan to manifest. Nature is a perfect example of timing and seasons. There are various seasons of planting and harvest that God has set. He sets the boundaries and times of the seasons, and they come and go. God has even orchestrated the best time for plants to be planted, and to grow, and then the time for them to be harvested. I am really amazed by the conditions that different plants and flowers grow best. In particular, there are some plants and trees that actually need fire in order to survive. A number of plants rely on fire to release their seeds, eliminate competition, or supply a rich layer of nutrient-filled ash. One example is the jack pine, found mostly in the very northern parts of the Central and Eastern U.S. and Canada. Their cones are very thick and hard. They are literally glued shut with a strong resin. These cones are referred to as serotinous cones, which means late blooming or opening.

Serotinous cones can hang on a pine tree for years without opening up to release their seeds. When a fire sweeps through a forest of jack pines, the heat from the fire melts the resin, allowing the cones to open up and release the seeds. Perhaps one of the most famous trees that have serotines cones are the giant redwood or sequoia trees of California. Their cones can contain up to 200 seeds and may take just under two years to mature. Once matured, they will remain in the cone and await a forest fire. The heat from the fire causes the cones to open and release their seeds.[6] If these plants were products of evolution, how did they evolve with their reliance on fire and smoke in order to survive? If it seems hard to believe, that's because it doesn't make sense scientifically. The only way plants could have a reliance on fire was for God to have designed them that way from the very beginning.

I am convinced that God has not only designed plants to be this way, but He has also equipped every one of His children to survive every season in there their life, during the time that He has appointed. The power of the Holy Spirit is living and dwelling inside of each of us. Our season will come, and the Holy Ghost fire will burn all of the hardness that is covering our hearts, allowing our seeds to burst. While you're waiting on your season, don't get jealous, don't be envious, and don't be stuck in your depression and lack of hope. "Do not get weary in your well doing, for in due season you shall reap if you faint not" (Galatians 6:9).

Praise Break

Prayer: Dear Heavenly Father, I thank you for this season of my life. Help me to embrace the God-appointed time that you have for my deliverance, my promotion, and my harvest. Give me strength to endure the cold and the hot seasons. Lord, remind me in the times that you have a reason for sending the rain, the sun, and the fire to help me to grow into the next stage of my life. I trust and believe in you, God, that you are the orchestrating every situation under the heavens, and it will work out for my good.

Scriptures:

Psalm 34:19:
Many are the afflictions of the righteous, But the LORD delivers him out of them all.

Isaiah 43:2:
When you pass through the waters, I will be with you; and when you pass through the rivers, they will not sweep over you. When you walk through the fire, you will not be burned; the flames will not set you ablaze.

I Peter 4:12-13:
Beloved, do not be surprised at the fiery ordeal among you, which comes upon you for your testing, as though some strange thing were happening to you; but to the degree that you share the sufferings of Christ, keep on rejoicing, so that also at the revelation of His glory you may rejoice with exultation.

Habakkuk 2:3:
For the vision is yet for an appointed time, but at the end it shall speak, and not lie: though it tarry, wait for it; because it will surely come, it will not tarry.

Chapter 4

Put It Away

◇◇◇◇◇◇◇◇◇◇◇◇◇◇◇◇◇◇◇◇◇◇◇◇◇◇◇

"When I was a child, I spake as a child, I understood as a child, I thought as a child: but when I became a man, I put away childish things."
—I Corinthians 13:11

I just recently celebrated my birthday. As I often do, I reflect on what I have done over the past year and see if I accomplished the goals that I feel should have been attainable by now. I also establish new goals for the next stage of my life. It often makes my husband nervous to have this reflective conversation with me. This year was certainly one that probably made him take several deep breaths. We were driving home from choir rehearsal, which by the way, is a treat for us to be in the same car. We are often being pulled between several different places with our jobs and the boys' travel basketball schedules, their school activities, and the ministry that we normally have to drive separately. Therefore, anytime there is a chance for us to actually be in the same car is a blessing. I have learned to enjoy the little moments because these moments add value to my life, and this night would prove to be of great value.

The weekend was approaching and my birthday fell on a Saturday that year. Our church has an annual Gospel Extravaganza the first weekend in June, and that means that this event can sometimes takes place on my birthday, as it did that year. The event is a big deal for our church, and the music ministry is heavily involved. Every member of the church is involved. We sell fish plates, bar-b-que, hot dogs, and ribs that the men cook. The women prepare the plates, run the service lines, and greet our guests. The youth have bouncy houses, games, cotton candy and snowball machines to keep them busy. We transform our parking lot and grass areas to an outdoor pavilion. We bring in a stage and sound, and our music ministries and liturgical dance groups minister to those in attendance.

I am one who believes that like no other day, your birthday should be the day that you get whatever you want. It is the day that you should not have to worry about what other people want; you get to eat where you want to, celebrate the way you want to celebrate, and be with who you want to be with—no questions asked. I am the person in our house who makes sure that you get your request on your birthday. I also feel most empowered on my birthday. In other words, I state what I want without any guilt whatsoever. I normally plan for how I want to celebrate my birthday. This year was different; I had not discussed anything with my family. Surely, I was not just going to go to the Gospel Extravaganza. As you might imagine, this had the potential to put my husband and the church's music minister in a precarious situation. Fortunately, however, he is a pro at marriage and church ministry tensions and balance. God had gifted us with time and space with the car ride together from choir practice.

Fernando, with wisdom and foresight, decided to have a touch-base time with me regarding my intentions for my birthday. I proceeded to tell him that I didn't know what I wanted to do. I expounded on the fact that I was disappointed in myself because I still had some behaviors, and what seemed to be lack of progress in some areas that I felt should have been met by now. Based on his past experiences with me, he asked me what was it that I felt like I should have accomplished by now. My inability to formulate a response was different. I became anxious; what would usually be a rapid response became a quiet, blubbering difficult articulation for me. This year, I could not state anything tangible that I wanted to accomplish or should have accomplished, like I have in the past, such as have a baby, be a principal, complete my doctorate, and so forth.

This year was more about my behavior. In fact, I said I am not disciplined, and I should have more discipline in some areas of my life. The best way to articulate my emotions boiled down to me saying, "I am too old to be acting this way." I should not still have the same limiting behaviors that I had before. I should be more progressive by now in my actions and my thoughts. Fernando gently but firmly responded to me that I was being too hard on myself. He expounded that while I should be pushing forward, he also recognized that I was not sitting idle and doing nothing; and the reason why I am not able to do the things that I wanted to do at the level that I wanted to do them on was because I need to increase my capacity. In other words, I needed to let some things go. I simply cannot have this expectation of myself to be performing or producing at the level that I wanted to without increasing my capacity to do them. Fernando's love and care for me in this moment reminded me of the scripture that I had read at my wedding, and I certainly heard it read at the majority of the weddings I have attended.

> *If I speak in the tongues of men or of angels, but do not have love, I am only a resounding gong or a clanging cymbal. If I have the gift of prophecy and can fathom all mysteries and all knowledge, and if I have a faith that can move mountains, but do not have love, I am nothing. If I give all I possess to the poor and give over my body to hardship that I may boast, but do not have love, I gain nothing. Love is patient, love is kind. It does not envy, it does not*

boast, it is not proud. It does not dishonor others, it is not self-seeking, it is not easily angered, and it keeps no record of wrongs. Love does not delight in evil but rejoices with the truth. It always protects, always trusts, always hopes, and always perseveres. Love never fails. But where there are prophecies, they will cease; where there are tongues, they will be stilled; where there is knowledge, it will pass away. For we know in part and we prophesy in part, but when completeness comes, what is in part disappears. When I was a child, I talked like a child, I thought like a child, I reasoned like a child. When I became a man, I put the ways of childhood behind me. For now we see only a reflection as in a mirror; then we shall see face to face. Now I know in part; then I shall know fully, even as I am fully known. And now these three remain: faith, hope and love. But the greatest of these is love.
—*1 Corinthians 13:1-13*

Fernando has been so patient with me through my many transitions and what I feel has been a moving target of goals. I feel like it's been a rollercoaster ride, but he makes sure that the ride is safe and fun. All I could think of was how much Fernando demonstrated the love that Paul was talking about in this scripture text. Paul was writing a letter to the church of Corinth. He had planted this church, and it was new in the faith. Now, just a few years later, he was receiving questioning letters and reports of problems. The church was troubled with division, lawsuits between believers, sexual sins, disorderly worship, and spiritual immaturity.

Paul wrote this uncompromising letter to correct these Christians, answer their questions, and instruct them in several areas. Paul was telling the people whom he loved that they needed to grow up. Paul starts off by reminding us of what love is all about, what it looks like, and how it should be the premise for how we are to treat one another. Then, Paul interrupts this instruction about love and starts to speak about a way of life when he says: "When I was a child, I spake as a child, I understood as a child, I thought as a child: but when I became a man, I put away childish things" (I Cor. 13:11).

Oftentimes when I heard this scripture spoken in isolation, as well as when it was said at weddings, I would equate this scripture as I no longer play with toys, I can take care of myself, I'm mature, I'm grown up, and therefore, all of those things that come with being grown have occurred. Looking deeper, I recognized that Paul said when I was a child I spake, understood, and thought like a child, he was talking about the system in which I approached life. In many ways and on several occasions, I began to recognize that in the way I was doing things, my systems were too small in speech, understanding, and thought for where God was trying to take me. Fernando was helping me realize that I was outgrowing my current way of doing things. I had to grow and create more room if I no longer wanted to feel tight. You have to have room to grow.

My reflection became different now. I begin to look at these three things that Paul stated and asked myself, "Is one of these areas stopping me from meeting my goals—is it what I am saying, is it the way I understand things, and is it my thinking that is stopping me from progressing? I needed to access my space for growth. I needed to monitor whether I was being loyal and crowding myself in a space and a system that was dysfunctional for this stage of my life. My system that lacked capacity was blocking my progress, and I didn't like what was happening. Fernando was right; I needed a new system that would enable me to increase my capacity to go to the next level of progress.

How could I increase capacity for speaking, thinking, and understanding? In order to change your way of speaking, understanding, and thinking you have to change your inner man, not your outward man. I am truly getting older in age and growing physically bigger in ways that I don't even want to discuss, but I am not growing the inner man as quickly as the outward man is growing. Take notice that Paul says, "When I became a man, I put away childish ways," not that I put away childish things and that made me a man. This is contradictory to the system and mindset that I was used to living under. Privileges and progress are normally tied to age. The older you get, the more things you should acquire. One of the reasons I think birthdays were big to me is my association with next steps and freedoms that come with being a certain age.

Growing up in a large family, I was the fifth out of six children, and we often equated acquiring privileges to becoming a certain age. I believe this helped my parents create some sense of balance, equity, and order in our house. For example, growing up in our parent's home, you could get baptized at age twelve, and my sisters and I could get our ears pierced at age thirteen. Our bedtimes, phone talk times, and chores were all tied to our ages. Society aids in embedding this rule of age and opportunity, as well. I have many examples that show how age determined my opportunities, privileges, and/or rights. At fifteen, one can get their learner's permit; at sixteen, their driver's license, at age eighteen, one can vote; at age twenty-one, a person is considered "legal" to purchase and consume alcohol; at age twenty-five, a person can rent a car; and then we hit a stretch in which there is nothing else that is directly age-driven until the age of sixty-five, when we can retire.

So, I am grown, I am no longer a child, I have hit all of the childhood marks, and I should be mature. However, I am not feeling mature at all. No longer is age a factor, and it is not providing me with any new privileges. The reason is because we are not talking about age any longer. Paul is not talking about age, and he is not talking about acquiring more things; he is referring to our spiritual being. I recognized that I was child in some spiritual areas of my life. There were areas in my life that I knew needed discipline, where I needed to grow up. I didn't like that I was still crying, still whining and pouting about the same things that I did last year in adult age.

I needed to build capacity. My feelings were spot on; I should have the desire to grow up and leave this state of infancy. What was Paul telling me to do? Paul was telling me to "put those childish ways aside," the way I speak, understand, and think. Paul ties together my desire with Fernando's desire for me to have more capacity. The way for me to grow up is that I have to lay some things down and let go of some things that may be stunting my growth. I can no longer operate within this childlike system of thinking, speaking and understanding and expect that I will create capacity in my life.

Paul said "I put it away." The system, the process, the person, whatever happening in your life can't put itself away, you have to put it away. You have the power to place whatever is under your authority. You do it, not your age, not your parents, not your spouse, but *you* put it away. One of my favorite educational theorists was John Dewey who believed that human beings learn through a hands-on approach. This places Dewey in the educational philosophy of pragmatism. Pragmatists believe that reality must be experienced. From Dewey's point of view, this means that students must interact with their environment to adapt and learn.[7] If I take the pragmatist's view of Dewey and the heart of a Christian, then I would understand that I would need to create a new experience, a new environment, for me to experience growth and development. There comes a time when you have to play with different toys and engage your hands, thoughts, and actions in areas that will develop you beyond your current situation. I was crying that I wanted to be in a different place, yet the reality was I was still playing on the same playground. I needed to stretch not only my desire to be more, but my willingness to be involved in conversations, partnerships, relationships, patterns, and readings that I had not engaged in before. Increasing does not mean taking things away, in fact, it is just the opposite; it means allow more to come into your life. My vision was so clouded by the all of the things that I had going on already that I couldn't see that I could not have a different experience without removing items on my to-do list or at least reprioritizing what was there.

I came to a place of understanding that just because I was developing space for new things to enter into my life; it didn't mean that everything from the past is gone. The people are still there, the tasks are still there, and sometimes the negative thinking, speaking, and understanding in childlike tendencies still existed. "Putting it away" doesn't mean that it left me; it is still there but I have put it in its rightful place. Therefore, it exists, and if I stay in it too long and continuously experience it, then it will do one of two things: I will limit it, or it will limit me. If I am not putting it away, then it is limiting me, and therefore, I am not growing. I have to take a deeper look at the each of these areas that Paul spoke about to see if they are limiting me or if I am limiting them.

When I was a child I spoke as a child.

Are my words limited like that of a child? How can I monitor the maturity of my speech? One approach that I would like to take is equating it to how researchers expect speech to develop in children. According to the research, "children typically speak their first word somewhere around 12 months. Some children, however, take up to 16 months to utter that long-awaited first word and this is still considered to be within the range of typical.

- At 18 months, children typically use around 50 words.
- At 24 months, children usually have an expressive vocabulary of 200–300 words.

- At 3 years, children can have anywhere from 500–1,100 words in their vocabulary.
- By 5–7 years, children have an expressive vocabulary of 3,000–5,000 words.[8]

It's important to note that when talking about vocabulary, we have to be careful to state what type of vocabulary we are looking at: *expressive vocabulary* (the number of words children use when they talk) or *receptive vocabulary* (which is the number of words children understand and that is almost always significantly higher than their expressive vocabulary). The above numbers represent expressive vocabulary, or the number of words children typically use at these ages. It's even more important to note that at least one study found that the significant variability in children's vocabulary at the age of three was strongly related to the amount of talking parents did with their children. Specifically, they found that parents who used "conversational" speech with their children (talking about what they did, what they saw, and what they thought about what they did and what they saw—basically just making conversation with their children on a regular and on-going basis) had children with significantly higher vocabularies and IQs at age three than children whose parents used mainly "directive" speech (get this, do that, come over here). [9]

There is a very good reason why I have given you these statistics around language and speech development in children. The difference between expressive and receptive vocabulary in your spiritual life is a part of your growth. Scripture tells us that life and death is in the power of the tongue. The Bible also says to speak those things as though they were. Knowing the difference between receptive vocabulary and expressive vocabulary, are you still speaking like a baby? When you understand what the Bible is saying, that is receptive vocabulary; and when you live out and speak what the Bible is saying, that is expressive vocabulary.

Does your receptive speech match your expressive speech? You may understand and be receptive to the scripture that "You can do all things through Christ Jesus who strengthens you," but your expressive speech says, "I can't do it." You may understand and be receptive to the ideas that the Bible says "God shall supply all of your needs according to his riches in glory," but your expressive language is: "I don't have it; I can't give more right now because the funds are not available." You may have receptive language and understand that the Word of God says "I will make you the head and not the tail, place you above and not beneath," but your expressive vocabulary is "I don't have the skills and the requirements necessary to get the promotion. They will never choose me. I am not smart enough, rich enough or educated enough."

I recognized that there was so much receptive vocabulary in my spiritual life that was not manifesting in my expressive language, and I had to increase my usage. I love the fact that research showed that the primary difference between the number of expressive vocabulary words used by some children over the others was not based on socioeconomic status, gender, or ethnicity; the difference in usage came from the amount of conversation parents were having with their children. If I needed to increase my expressive language, then I needed to remind myself that salvation is also free. Just like words, it was not determined by my socioeconomic status, gender, or ethnicity. I can grow just from the practice and being around those who are using the spiritual words and principles around me. The study goes on to give the following tips to parents who want to increase their toddler's vocabulary. I want to take the suggestions below and reapply them to your spiritual growth in expressive language.

1. "At the toddler age, use simple language to talk about what you and your child are seeing and doing. Narrate your day and engage your child in simple back and forth

conversations about what is happening."[10] Go back to reciting the scriptures that you know. Learning the Lord's Prayer, the Ten Commandments, or maybe even quoting your favorite Bible verse for the day. Read a daily devotional and scripture each day. Most importantly, begin to look at all the blessings and gifts that God has given you on a daily basis and speak them out loud in thankfulness. We take it as just rhetoric when we hear a testimony that starts with "Thank you, Lord, for waking me up this morning, for starting me on my way, for giving me food to eat and shoes on my feet." However, this may be the place to begin expressing your thankfulness, and it is very worthy to be spoken because we have been given far more than what our expressive language ever gives voice to. One of Satan's primary tools used to distract us is to place in our minds all of the things that we don't have and tempt us to give expressive voice to those things. Instead, we have to be very intentional about flipping the table and start speaking all of the things that we have, and as your faith grows, start speaking to the things that you know are promised to you. This leads us to the second recommendation given to improve the amount of expressive language.

2. "Think about taking pictures and using them to extend and repeat the conversation about events that have happened, even with children as young as 24 months. Talking about things that have already happened helps your child learn to talk about decontextualized events (things that are not right in front of him)—a task that requires a more precise and higher-level vocabulary."[11]

If Satan could get you to forget what God has already done for you, he would certainly try to do that right off the gate. Therefore, sometimes we encourage people to keep a journal, keep a picture, or revisit a post from Instagram or Facebook to remind them, but more importantly once they recall whatever it is, they need to tell somebody, which is another important reason to have testifying services. Although we may have different means of giving and hearing testimonies, the spirit of it is the same. You don't have to have a formal devotional service to tell others what God has done for you. You can call a friend and share the news, or you can send a simple tweet or a post on any other social media platform to tell of the goodness of Jesus. The important factor is that you are telling others that you are diving deep into your day, into the moments to remind yourself and to witness to others that God is a part of your life and is still supplying us with this great gift of the present day. The need to share with others is not only beneficial for your own growth, but others depend on it as well and that brings us to the next tip given to increase our expressive language.

3. As your child develops language in their preschool and elementary years, continue to engage him in conversations about things that have happened in your lives. When you do so, use active listening to show your child you are listening and create opportunities for your child to comment and add to your thoughts. Create pockets of time in which you really talk with your child.[12] Sometimes we don't have the words to say, we have not experienced the situation, and we have no reference because the people that are speaking to us on a daily basis are not using this level of vocabulary. Therefore, increase your exposure to the right expressive vocabulary from those who do know. Read the Word of God and study the scriptures through a Bible study, listen to other people's testimonies to help increase your faith, and find mentors (they can be informal) that are specializing in the language that you need to grow.

When I was a child I understood as a child.

My frustrations with my lack of growth primarily had to do with my lack of understanding. I didn't understand that age didn't equate to spiritual growth and maturity. I was running out of tangible targets and goals that were age-based. The Word of the Lord says "Wisdom is the principal thing; therefore get wisdom: and with all thy getting, get understanding" (Prov. 4:7). These were not material things that the Lord wanted me to get; He said to get an understanding. We have heard all of the sayings, such as knowledge is power and seek first to understand than to be understood. Some define understanding as the truth you stand under. If that is the case, then that means you determine what is right and what is wrong. You set the rules and apply them to your version of understanding. Understanding is not a simple task no matter the content. Understanding gets especially complicated when we are trying to understand who we are and is almost overwhelming in a growth period when you are trying to understand who God is calling you to be.

Gaining understanding requires reflective work and constant communication with God through prayer, scripture, and meditation. To gain understanding is not stopping at a yes or a no, but going beyond the surface and diving deep into the reasoning. Understanding is all personal work; it involves one asking themselves questions, such as: Do I really understand what God is calling me to do? Have I spent enough time to listen and not cast judgements from those who may be different from me in opinion and thought? Do I understand that God has an appointed time to manifest in the natural? Do I have a sincere desire to seek understanding through direct holy communion prayer and consecrated time with God in my daily life?

A childish way of gaining understanding is to depend on others to tell you. Like a child, you can ask for your direction from others, like your mother, father, the preacher, and social media platforms. All of these people can be used to carry a message of God. These people can help you formulate clarity and add to your development. However, all of these people have a limit on their understanding of who God is calling you to be, and just like me, they have opinions that may not align with God's plan for you. Maturing in the area of understanding is more about you listening to God about your life instead of you listening to others about your life. Mature understanding is having the ability to see past the moment and look toward the greater goal. Mature understanding is waiting on the Lord to reveal Himself. Mature understanding requires a transformation of your mind.

Praise Break

Prayer: God thank you for giving me the wisdom to understand the things that I cannot change; and the courage to change the things that I can change. Lord, I ask that You continue to give me the strength to put away all of the thoughts, words, and actions that are keeping me from reaching my divine destiny. Today Lord, I commit to growing in a mature knowledge and understanding of who I am in Christ. Today, I seek to please God and not man.

Scriptures:

Galatians 5:16-18
But I say, walk by the Spirit, and you will not carry out the desire of the flesh. For the flesh sets its desire against the Spirit, and the Spirit against the flesh; for these are in opposition to one another, so that you may not do the things that you please. But if you are led by the Spirit, you are not under the Law.

Colossians 3:9-10
Do not lie to one another, since you laid aside the old self with its evil practices, and have put on the new self who is being renewed to a true knowledge according to the image of the One who created him—

Galatians 5:25
If we live by the Spirit, let us also walk by the Spirit.

Ephesians 4:22-24
that, in reference to your former manner of life, you lay aside the old self, which is being corrupted in accordance with the lusts of deceit, and that you be renewed in the spirit of your mind, and put on the new self, which in the likeness of God has been created in righteousness and holiness of the truth.

Romans 6:6
knowing this, that our old self was crucified with Him, in order that our body of sin might be done away with, so that we would no longer be slaves to sin;

1 Peter 2:1
Therefore, putting aside all malice and all deceit and hypocrisy and envy and all slander,

1 Peter 1:14
As obedient children, do not be conformed to the former lusts which were yours in your ignorance,

1Peter 2:24
and He Himself bore our sins in His body on the cross, so that we might die to sin and live to righteousness; for by His wounds you were healed.

1 John 1:6-7

If we say that we have fellowship with Him and yet walk in the darkness, we lie and do not practice the truth; but if we walk in the Light as He Himself is in the Light, we have fellowship with one another, and the blood of Jesus His Son cleanses us from all sin.

Chapter 5

Positioning for Godly Transformation

◇◇◇◇◇◇◇◇◇◇◇◇◇◇◇◇◇◇◇◇◇◇◇◇

"And be not conformed to this world: but be ye transformed by the renewing of your mind, that ye may prove what is that good, and acceptable, and perfect will of God."

—*Romans 12:2*

The New Testament Greek word for "transformed" is *metamorphoō*. This word denotes change resulting from forces beyond one's own effort or power. A godly transformation is genuinely God-achieved and God-sustained, requiring no effort on our part to attain it or live it out. When we know the truth in our hearts, we will be renewed and live differently from that point forward— with little to no effort. When we experience a godly transformation, Jesus is living His life in and through us; therefore we speak like Him, we have an understanding like Him, and we think and act just like Jesus. Therefore, we will pour out the fruits of His spirit.

The transformation process that is taking place in you can be compared to the metamorphosis that occurs when a caterpillar is transformed into a butterfly. The process that butterfly goes through to get from its caterpillar state to its butterfly state requires little to no effort from the butterfly. The butterfly does not expend any personal energy or effort in the transformation. Once the transformation occurs, the butterfly is a new creation and does not need to work to maintain its transformation. Instead, the butterfly works to stay alive and reproduce. It is the same for us as Christians. God has changed us, and we are new creatures; the problem is not that we are not butterflies—we are human adults. The challenge is staying alive and reproducing more fruit. This is why we have to think like we are truly transformed.

The butterfly goes through four stages of transformation that we can compare to our own godly transformation. The first stage is *the egg*. A butterfly starts life as a very small, round, oval or cylindrical egg. The coolest thing about butterfly eggs, especially monarch butterfly eggs, is that if you look closely enough, you can actually see the tiny caterpillar growing inside of it.[13] God created every one of us this way; we start out as an egg. We are small in our physical size, our thoughts, and in our speaking. The beautiful and miraculous work of God is that He knows exactly, even before this stage of the egg, that you are going to be great. "Before I formed you in the womb I knew you, before you were born, I set you apart; I appointed you as a prophet to the nations" (Jer. 1:5). When we change our thinking, we understand that even though I am physically small, I am still the king or queen that God has destined, appointed, me to be. Dr. Tiffany A. Little is still daddy's baby girl, Tiffy, Tiffy Lynn, Tiffany Alston, Mrs. Tiffany Alston Little, Minster Little. The egg is the same; the reception of me and the service that I give is what changed.

The second stage is *the larva*. When the egg finally hatches, most of you would expect for a butterfly to emerge, right? Well, not exactly. Butterfly larvae are actually what we call caterpillars. Caterpillars do not stay in this stage for very long and mostly, in this stage, all they do is eat. When the egg hatches, the caterpillar will start his work and eat the leaf they were born onto. When they start eating, they instantly start growing and expanding.

Their exoskeleton (skin) does not stretch or grow, so they grow by "molting" (shedding the outgrown skin) several times while it grows.[14] Just as I started to shed some of my childhood names and took on new names, so did my ways of living my life. Not only did my name change from Tiffany Alston to Tiffany Little, but where I lived changed and my way of life changed. I became a wife and mother. I started to read books and articles about being a good wife and mother. In fact, at every stage of expansion, the growth comes from your intake, what you are eating. The mothers of the caterpillars are very aware of this; thus the reason why they work hard to place the eggs on good leaves, leaves that will nourish the caterpillars. The more you grow in knowledge, the less time you have for foolishness. Like the caterpillar, you begin to outgrow this way of life, and day by day, you start to shed some layers off. This is the stage when I started to shed the negative thoughts, the dependence on others, and the need for validation and continued to eat up positivity and who I was becoming in Christ.

It is important to recognize that you are in this stage. If not, you will stay here, no growth will take place, and if you don't grow, then eventually you will die. This may be why the Lord will allow us to become uncomfortable. In fact, you become enslaved to this state. You stay a child. Galatians 4:1–2 states, "Now I say, that the heir, as long as he is a child, differed nothing from a servant. Though he be Lord of all. But he is under tutors, governors, until the time appointed of the father." There is a reason why you feel too big for the space you are in, and that is because you know that God has something greater for you. However, this scripture tells us that you can't operate in your lordship if you are still in a space and area that is conducive to a child. God will not appoint you to the position until you have matured in your spiritual development. You will remain under the supervision of people who you should be leading. However, if you continue to ignore the growth and deny that you need to let some things go, then you will suffocate in this space. If you don't put it away, then it will put you away. Leave this place so that you can go to your palace. Let go so that you can go into your next season.

The third stage is *the pupa*. As soon as a caterpillar is done growing and they have reached their full length/weight, they form themselves into a pupa, also known as a chrysalis. From the outside of the pupa, it looks as if the caterpillar may just be resting, but the inside is where all of the action is. Inside the pupa, the caterpillar is changing rapidly. As I began to grow my spiritual man, it was important, like the caterpillar, to wrap myself in the Word of God, immerse myself in the scripture, and to honestly get a place away from everyone. I needed to let the Lord work on my heart and hear from him and only Him. Godly transformation began to happen in my life.

The chrysalis stage is where on the outside it looks like nothing is going on or nothing is happening, but really there is a lot going on. In this stage of godly transformation, God is doing a mighty operation on the inside. This is the place that seems to be dark and covered up, but God loves to develop in the dark. I understand now in this stage that I was no longer afraid of the dark because I shed that layer of fear. In fact, I was like a Polaroid picture at this point being developed in a dark room. When God's light started to hit me, I was transformed into the work of art that God has created for me to be.

I close my ears in this place because the devil would have me believe that nothing is going on because no one can see the process. Trust strongly in the scripture when it says, "But as it is written, Eye hath not seen, nor ear heard, neither have entered into the heart of man, the things which God hath prepared for them that love him" (I Corinthians 2:9). Now that I have spent some time with God growing and transforming into the heart of Christ, I should now know who I am in Christ. No longer should I think like and operate like a caterpillar—a transformation has occurred. As a caterpillar, my thinking was short, stubby, and had no wings at all. Within the chrysalis, my old body parts as a caterpillar were undergoing a remarkable transformation. The tissue, limbs, and organs of a caterpillar have all been changed by the time the pupa is finished and is now ready for the final stage to become a butterfly.

Finally, the caterpillar has done all of its forming and changing inside the pupa. When the butterfly first emerges from the chrysalis, both of the wings are soft and folded against its body. This is because the butterfly had to fit all its new parts inside of the pupa. As soon as the butterfly has rested after coming out of the chrysalis, it will pump blood into the wings to get them working and flapping—and then, it gets to fly. In education, and at our school in particular, we use the phrase *make your thinking visible*. Math teachers will tell you to show your work; in other words, show me how you arrived at the answer to the problem. Again, Paul reminds us that a complete transformation happens with the renewal of the mind. Therefore, you will know that you have been transformed when you can "show me your thinking." The adult butterfly not only shows us physically that it has reached the stage of transformation through the outward appearance, but the butterfly, through its actions, shows us that it is now an adult. When in the fourth and final stage of their lives, adult butterflies are constantly on the lookout to reproduce, and when a female lays their eggs on some leaves, the butterfly life cycle will start all over again. When you have been transformed, you produce. You start looking for the next person to pour into. You start making disciples. You begin to make your thinking visible. You begin to tell people about Jesus and all that He has done for you in your life.

You used to think that once this person walked out of your life that you would never make it. You used to think that the death of a loved one would keep you depressed and lost without them. You used to think that the loss of job would mean the end of your financial stability. You used to think that your wrongdoings would keep you shackled, locked up, and imprisoned. You used to think that your disability, inability, and lack thereof would keep you from divine destiny. But now you are transformed by renewing of your mind, and you are making your thinking visible by evidence of your worship. You look like a butterfly now—a Christian whose worship is real. Your transformation is visible in your worship. You can praise God in every stage because you know that God is with you, will never leave you and will never forsake you. This is what God desires for us: transformation that changes us into something we cannot become on our own. This is where the fruit of the Spirit is made manifest.

Praise Break

Prayer: Lord, I make our thinking visible by lifting my voice in thanksgiving and clapping my hands in praise because through it all, I have learned to trust in you, Jesus. Lord, I praise you because no matter what stage I am in, you are doing a mighty work of transformation in my life. Lord, continue to build me in the formation that you have designed for my life. Lord, continue to remove the layers of waste from my life so that I can increase capacity in my life to do the work that you have called me to do. Lord, thank you for being my Prince of Peace, my Everlasting Father. I praise you, I praise you, I praise you, I praise you, Lord, for I am fearfully and wonderfully made.

Scriptures:

Romans 8:38–39:
For I am sure that neither death nor life, nor angels nor rulers, nor things present nor things to come, nor powers, nor height nor depth,

nor anything else in all creation, will be able to separate us from the love of God in Christ Jesus our Lord.

Deuteronomy 31:6:
Be strong and courageous. Do not fear or be in dread of them, for it is the Lord your God who goes with you. He will not leave you or forsake you.

John 3:16 King James Version (KJV):
For God so loved the world, that he gave his only begotten Son, that whosoever believeth in him should not perish, but have everlasting life.

Romans 8:35–39 King James Version (KJV):
Who shall separate us from the love of Christ? shall tribulation, or distress, or persecution, or famine, or nakedness, or peril, or sword? As it is written, for thy sake we are killed all the day long; we are accounted as sheep for the slaughter.

Nay, in all these things we are more than conquerors through him that loved us.

For I am persuaded, that neither death, nor life, nor angels, nor principalities, nor powers, nor things present, nor things to come,

Nor height, nor depth, nor any other creature, shall be able to separate us from the love of God, which is in Christ Jesus our Lord.

Proverbs 4:5–9 King James Version (KJV):
Get wisdom, get understanding: forget it not; neither decline from the words of my mouth.
Forsake her not, and she shall preserve thee: love her, and she shall keep thee.

Wisdom is the principal thing; therefore get wisdom: and with all thy getting get understanding.

Proverbs 23:7 King James Version (KJV):
For as he thinketh in his heart, so is he: Eat and drink, saith he to thee; but his heart is not with thee.

Chapter 6
You've Got to Move

◇◇◇◇◇◇◇◇◇◇◇◇◇◇◇◇◇◇◇◇◇◇◇◇◇◇◇◇◇

> *"The Lord said to Moses, "Why do you cry to me? Tell the people of Israel to go forward. Lift up your staff, and stretch out your hand over the sea and divide it, that the people of Israel may go through the sea on dry ground."*
> —*Exodus 14:15–16*

There is no doubt that God has worked miracles in my life. I know that my desire to be more and do more for Christ is stronger than it has ever been before. I have a transformed heart, attitude and mind. At this point in life, one would think that moving forward would be easy, especially when you are moving to something greater. However, the problem is the enemy knows that you are moving to something greater as well. Moses knew that God had something greater for him and the Israelites, but they didn't seem to want to move forward to get to the blessed Promised Land. One of the reasons is that the enemy devises attacks that will cause you to want to stop in your tracks and not move forward. Satan is well aware that where you are going will be a place where you will be free and no longer enslaved to him. Therefore, the devil would certainly like for you to stay right where you are—under his rule.

Satan wants you stuck, head down, and working for him. He wants you to have no vision, no hope, no peace, no strength, and no desire. It is his number one goal to stop you in your tracks to progress. Satan knows that he can't stop the promise, so he has to stop you from getting to the promise. Thus, he wants you to choose not to move forward. Satan wants you to do what the Israelites were tempted to do; he wants you to stay in place and either serve as his slave or die. He wants to stop you from moving.

Many of us know the familiar story of Moses and the parting of the Red Sea. God chose Moses to lead the Israelites out of slavery in Egypt into the land of Canaan, which God had promised to them. Initially the Israelites were all onboard with Moses and followed their wonderful leader. Often, it is not hard for us to accept the promise that God has given to us. We are excited about the potential of where we are going, but we are weary of the process it takes to get to where we are going. It reminds me of a very bad habit that I have when it comes to weight loss. I have probably engaged with at least three personal trainers and/or some type of weight loss program, and with each one, I am drawn in by the promise that if I follow the training and eating regiment, I will get to a healthy and ideal body weight.

I listen to the trainers, the leaders of the programs, and I am all excited and buy into the promise. The promise makes sense. I can tell that it is possible to achieve my goal because they give me all kinds of research and even examples of others for whom it has worked, and I am totally all into moving forward with the plan. I even noticed that trainers and these programs most of the time have had me pay upfront. I realize now why they do; they do this because as soon as an obstacle seems to present itself, I forget the promise and stop moving. There is a required effort from me to get this goal. Therefore, the trainers are hoping that if I invest my financial resources into the process, then hopefully, I will think twice about staying stuck in my place. So, what does the enemy do? He sends me physical pain and soreness to make me stop. He creates scheduling conflicts to make me stop; he tries everything every time to get me to stop moving forward.

Pharaoh did the same thing when he heard that the Israelites were trying to move forward. As soon as Pharaoh heard about the Israelites leaving, he decided to seek after the Israelites with chariots, and he caught up with and surrounded them at Pi-hahiroth. The Bible provides us with some points of interest regarding the position of the camp of Israel.

The positioning of the camp of Israel:

1. Scripture says that Israel came to a dead end at Etham, then God told them to turn back and retrace their steps and camp directly beside the "Migdol" in order for Pharaoh to say, "Now the Lord spoke to Moses, saying, 'Tell the sons of Israel to turn back and camp before Pi-hahiroth, between Migdol and the sea; you shall camp in front of Baal-zephon, opposite it, by the sea. For Pharaoh will say of the sons of Israel, They are wandering aimlessly in the land; the wilderness has shut them in. Thus I will harden Pharaoh's heart, and he will chase after them; and I will be honored through Pharaoh and all his army, and the Egyptians will know that I am the Lord." And they did so. Exodus 14:1–4
2. Pi-hahiroth means a "mouth of water" in Hebrew. Notice that "Pi-hahiroth faces Baal-zephon" in Numbers 33:7. If you look at the "mouth" it indeed faces Baal-zephon.
3. Exodus 14:2: Tell the sons of Israel to turn back and camp before Pi-hahiroth, between Migdol and the sea; you shall camp in front of Baal-zephon, opposite it, by the sea.
4. Numbers 33:7: They journeyed from Etham and turned back to Pi-hahiroth, which faces Baal-zephon, and they camped before Migdol.[15]

How do you move when the enemy is encamped all around you? You have heard the promise, but the enemy feels so close and so overbearing with his 600 chariots and fancy equipment to overtake you and to knock you down. How do you move when you find yourself unmotivated and despondent about what you're trying to achieve? How can you move forward? There was no doubt that the Israelites were trapped and that seemed even more problematic was that they were trapped due to a redirection from God. Sometimes in order to get to the place that God has promised you, it will feel like He is taking you backwards. It sometimes even feels like a setup. I know this feeling so well; it seemed that as soon as I had gone through the most difficult parts of my professional journey, completed my educational doctorate, and my work trajectory was geared toward a superintendent position. And just like that, God seemed to redirect me back to where I first began—as a classroom teacher.

I was just like the Israelites; I believed in the promise, but I couldn't see past the attacks of the enemy. The first thing I was tempted to do was to blame others and/or my current circumstances. I also began to question whether this was really the way that God was leading me. The Israelites asked Moses, "Why did you bring us here to die; were there no graves in Egypt?" They could not see past this huge problem and basically said we could have just stayed as slaves in Egypt instead of dying in the wilderness. Oftentimes, this is what happens; we would rather stay in this state of slavery. We become the least productive manifestation of ourselves and begin focusing on anger, frustration, and anxiety. We paralyze ourselves, and if we are not careful, we will begin to accept the death the enemy offers and not the promise of God. We stay put and don't move forward, waiting for the devil to kill us, without a fight. So, what do we do when we can't move forward, when we say we are stuck in a rut?

Change Your Environment

Psychologist provide some steps that you can take to help you move forward. The first two steps involve you changing your state or your current environment. For example, if you have been inside all day, maybe you should go out and get some sun. Do something different than your normal routine. One thing that I love about the Bible so much is that it remains relevant—what worked in the biblical times is still working today, and in actuality, we are just scratching the surface with the knowledge and wisdom comes from the Bible. Whether the Israelites knew it or not, Moses had to change their environment. He had to take them from the place that they were used to being in and bring them to another place. It's amazing but simple; if you stay in the place where you were a slave, then you will continue to act like a slave. In the conditions there, you naturally yield to the same behavior. As long as they stayed in Egypt under Pharaoh, they would continue to stay slaves as they admitted: "Is not this what we said to you in Egypt: 'Leave us alone that we may serve the Egyptians. For it would have been better for us to serve the Egyptians than to die in the wilderness'" (Exod. 14:12). You have to move into a different space and train yourself differently if you want something different in your life.

Athletes are trained and conditioned by doing what they call reps—repetitions of different exercises and activities several times over. They do this so that they can develop what they call muscle memory. So, for a basketball player, it will mean that every time I get the basketball, I am going to shoot it with this form. I am conditioned this way every time I see a basketball net; it's natural for me to play the game in this way. Another example is the one that people would tell me when I went to college. I can remember everyone telling me that you shouldn't study or work in your bed because that is where you sleep, and your body will naturally begin to think you should fall asleep. The opposite could also happen that if you are beginning to make your bed your workplace; then you will change the purpose of the bed and no longer will be able to rest in it.

God had to change the location, and although they were in the wilderness, this was all a part of God's plan. Sometimes we have to stop complaining that God moved us to the wilderness and instead start praising Him for the wilderness because it will be in the wilderness that He is going to do His mighty work in your life. He is changing our environment for a reason.

Take Ownership

We live in a "who's to blame" society. Parents blame the educators, the educators blame the parents. The Republicans blame the Democrats, the Democrats blame the Republicans. The rich blame the poor, the poor blame the rich. I can't even go to a faith-based meeting or speak with faith-based leaders without someone placing blame. There is opposition and blame in every rough situation. Everyone wants credit for the good, but nobody wants to own the bad. This second step acknowledges that we have a responsibility as citizens, as educators, as parents and, most importantly, as Christians to take some ownership of the plight of man that we are seeing and experiencing. Most of all, we fail to understand that we own our destinies. God gives us a choice to accept the lies of the enemy or to take control of our situations by asking God to come into this process, to guide and lead us. We forget to stop pointing fingers toward others and instead start lifting our hands up toward our help, the source of all our needs. We stay focused on the problem, instead of God—the one and only solution.

Some of us stay focused on the guilt of our shame; and we even buy into the lie that we deserve less than the promise of God. We begin to believe that we deserve to be broken, abused, and enslaved. We start to sound like the Israelites—we should have just stayed slaves. Today we would say that if we didn't protest, if we didn't speak up for what was right, then maybe our young black boys would not be dying. We should have made them stay home. It sounds like we should have kept our schools segregated; then at least we would have teachers who treated and talked to our children equitably and would not have a disproportionate rate of black and brown children labeled with learning disabilities and suspended at higher rates that than their white counterparts. Today it sounds like: "I will not speak up for injustice at my workplace or speak truth because then I will no longer be popular," or "I may lose a contract, customer or my job, so I just remain politically correct and stay a slave to policy and worse yet, to myself." It looks like behavior that embraces and accepts abusive relationships, abusive government systems, and abusive work environments. At this point, we are no longer buying into the promise; instead we act like the Israelites and buy into that speech of "this is just the way it is," and we decide not to fight back with the right weapons of prayer and praise. We choose to stay in this place of negativity by casting blame. In order to move from this state, you have to shift your focus to the promises of God, reflecting on his goodness.

"Yet this I call to mind and therefore I have hope. Because of the Lord's great love, we are not consumed for his compassion never fail. They are new every morning; great is your faithfulness" (Lam. 3:21–23). One of the tricks of the enemy is to try to take away your joy. He does this by occupying your mind with the pains of today and the worries of tomorrow. But the prophet reminds us in this scripture that when we think back about what the Lord has already done, then we should have hope. God has been faithful, and his mercy has never failed. And so Moses, too, reminded the Israelites to "Fear not, stand firm, and see the salvation of the Lord, which he will work for you today. For the Egyptians you see today, you shall never see again. The Lord will fight for you and you have only to be silent" (Exod. 14:13). Moses reminds us that our God will fight for you. God is going to get the glory, and you shall have the victory. There is just one thing that is the way of victory, and contrary to popular belief, it's not the Red Sea. It's not your struggle. What is keeping you from your victory is your non-movement. In order for one to get to victory, one must move to it. You can't get the victory if you don't move forward. You can't move forward if you are still lingering in the past.

Letting Go of the Past

We have to leave the past behind us. It's no wonder that the third step of letting go of your past is what is suggested to get you toward your goal. Scripture tells us to remember Lot's wife. Lot's family was living in Sodom. It was such a cesspool of iniquity that God said He would destroy it. But, because of Lot's presence in the city, Abraham interceded for its preservation. The Lord, however, couldn't find two righteous people, so He said, "I will still destroy the city but deliver Lot's family." The Lord sent two angels to come and deliver Lot and his family from the terrible judgment that was about to fall on Sodom. As the story goes, when the fire and brimstone fell out of heaven onto Sodom, Lot's wife looked back from behind her husband. It was the custom of the land that the wife would walk some distance from her husband. However, Lot's wife did more than just walk behind him, she lingered and looked back, and because she tarried, she was overtaken by the vapors, encrusted with salt, and perished where she stood. Lot's wife didn't want to leave the city. This was the only city that she knew; this was the only life that she had ever known. She loved Sodom so much that when the angel of mercy sought to save her from the angel of judgment, she could not be saved. In that look back to Sodom was regret for all she was leaving for an unknown life before her, and as she sighed, the salt air whitened her body into marble, and "nature made for her at once a grave and a monument." Lot's wife let her past be her destiny.

I remind you to remember Lot's wife. You don't want to be so consumed and so tied up in the things of the world, in the past, that you can't go to your future. You can't grieve and mourn the loss of the things, the people, or the sinful ways of life that God is telling you to leave behind and expect to get to your Promised Land; if you stay back, you will die in that very place. You can't be like Lot's wife and hear the word and voice of God speaking to you but ignore the word. This may have been the only way you have lived, but when God is telling you to move, you must move. "Escape for thy life, look not behind thee ... lest thou be consumed."

Don't be consumed; instead listen to the Lord. He has a plan for deliverance. He sees the tears, He knows the pain, and He is well aware of your struggles. In fact, he said to Moses, "Why do you cry to me? Tell the people of Israel to go forward" (Exod. 14:15). God is a forward-moving God; God is our refuge and strength, a very present help in the time of trouble. As the story continues, Moses was commanded by God to hold his staff out over the water, and throughout the night, a strong east wind divided the sea, and the Israelites passed through with a wall of water on either side. The Egyptians pursued, but at dawn, God clogged their chariot wheels and threw them into a panic, and with the return of the water, Pharaoh and his entire army were destroyed. Here is what happens when you do the opposite of Lot's wife, when you don't look back but you move forward. God will demonstrate miraculous, wonder-working power in your life. Oftentimes, we are so fixed on the one thorn in our side, the one obstacle that stands in our way, but God is great and He is mighty. He is not going just for the one thorn; He is going for the entire bush. You think that you have the plan to fight one enemy, but God is going to take down the entire kingdom.

Why is it necessary? Why are the Christians having to go through the wilderness? Why does it seem like the Satan is ruling? Those may all be perfectly good questions that you are asking. God made it clear when He said, "I will let them rise up against you because when they come after you, I will destroy them, and all of them will know that I am the Lord." We can start to praise God right here. The Lord wants you to know if you are in the wilderness that He is about to do something so powerful, so great, that He will destroy everything around you that tries to attack you—everything that tries to come up against your family destroyed, every attack on your body destroyed, every attack on your marriage destroyed. God said He would destroy this entire system, this entire operation. He is God! "What manner of man is this that seas obey, what manner of man is this that even the winds obey." God is the maker. He created the heavens and the earth, and God can do exactly what He wants to do it, how He wants to do it, when He wants to do it. He is the great I AM. This is why you can move forward to your divine destiny.

I'm reminded of the story of Deborah who lived in the mountainous region of Ephraim, between the towns of Bethel and Ramah. There she would sit beneath a palm tree and serve the people as Jehovah directed. Her assignment was surely challenging, but Deborah did not allow it to daunt her. There was a dire need for her services. The people were unfaithful. "They chose new gods; then there was war in the gates" (Judges 5:8). Because the Israelites left Jehovah to serve other gods, Jehovah abandoned them to their enemies. Canaanite King Jabin dominated them, using a mighty general named Sisera. Under his rule, the Canaanite religion and culture were brutal, featuring child sacrifice and temple prostitution. Deborah's song reveals that travel was nearly impossible in the land, and village life had all but ended. "In the days of Shamgar the son of Anath, in the days of Jael, the highways were unoccupied, and the travelers walked through byways. The inhabitants of the villages ceased, they ceased in Israel, until I, Deborah, arose, that I arose a mother in Israel" (Judges 5-7). We may imagine people cowering in the woods and hills, afraid to farm and terrified to travel on the open roads lest they be attacked, their children taken, and their women raped. Does it sound like a place you know, a similar situation going on in our country now? Unfortunately, sometimes history does truly repeat itself.

The scripture says that terror reigned for twenty years until Deborah decided to get up and move forward. The book of Judges states, "The inhabitants of the villages ceased, they ceased in Israel, until I, Deborah, arose, that I arose a mother in Israel." Not only does the enemy not want you to get your blessing and reach your destiny, but he knows that if you don't move, he can stop an entire city or nation from prospering. Your forward movement is not just for your good, but it is for the good of an entire nation. God is calling you to rise up and be the mothers and the fathers of this land. Moving may look like leaving your comfort zone. You may have to go through the wilderness, but I encourage you to not look back on things in your past. Instead, do as Paul stated: "Brethren, I count not myself to have apprehended but this one thing I do, forgetting those things which are behind, and reaching forth unto those things which are before, I press toward the mark for the prize of the high calling of God in Christ Jesus" (Phil. 3:13–14) Your destiny, your Promised Land, your prize, is before you, not behind you, but you must move to your blessing. As the late great Dr. Martin Luther King stated: "If you can't fly, then run; if you can't run, then walk; if you can't walk, then crawl; but whatever you do, you have to keep moving forward."

Praise Break

Prayer: Lord, I have seen the power of God, and therefore I put my faith in Him. I will continue to run this race, with my head high and my arms extended and moving forward. Just as the Israelites sung a song of praise to the Lord for the crossing of the sea, I sing songs of praise for the provisions He has made, the doors He has opened, and the seas that He has helped me to cross. I understand the hymnist when he wrote now: "My hope is built on nothing less than Jesus blood and righteousness, I dare not trust the sweetest frame, but wholly lean on Jesus' name. On Christ, the solid rock I stand, all other ground is sinking sand, all other ground is sinking sand."

Scriptures:

Deuteronomy 31:8:
The LORD himself goes before you and will be with you; he will never leave you nor forsake you. Do not be afraid; do not be discouraged.

Isaiah 43:2:
When you pass through the waters, I will be with you; and when you pass through the rivers, they will not sweep over you. When you walk through the fire, you will not be burned; the flames will not set you ablaze.

Job 17:9:
The righteous keep moving forward, and those with clean hands become stronger and stronger.

Philippians 3:14:
I run straight I run toward the goal to win the prize that God's heavenly call offers in Christ Jesus.

Proverbs 4:18:
The way of the righteous is like the first gleam of dawn, which shines ever brighter until the full light of day.

Psalm 1:2-3:
Instead he finds pleasure in obeying the Lord's commands; he meditates on his commands day and night. He is like a tree planted by flowing streams; it yields its fruit at the proper time, and its leaves never fall off. He succeeds in everything he attempts.

Psalm 119:104-105:
I obtain understanding from your precepts; therefore I hate every false way. Your word is a lamp for my feet, a light for my pathway.

Proverbs 6:23:
For this command is a lamp, this teaching is a light, and correction and instruction are the way to life,

Chapter 7
Moving from Fear to Faith

"Don't fear, for I have redeemed you; I have called you by name; you are Mine."
—Isaiah 43:1

Fernando and I knew that it was going to be a leap of faith to move back to Charlotte. But the great news was that we were moving forward, and we were not looking back. We knew that there were several things we needed that God was going to have to go before us and work on our behalf. In fact, initially I was very excited and not worried at all about returning to a school district that I had left in good standing. There seemed to be many opportunities that were before both Fernando and me that appeared very promising. However, as time went by and the opportunities were either not immediately available or not offered to me, fear began to creep into my heart. Fear is different from doubt. I didn't doubt that the Lord would provide or that this was the right decision to move back. No, I didn't doubt and I recognized that I feared that I would not be able to sustain and make it work until the Lord did provide. I reached out to my dad, as I often do for spiritual council, and told him my concerns. My dad spoke to me in his usual prophetic way, and said to me, "Everything that you do from now on will be done through and by faith." I pondered over this for a while, trying to dissect every part of what this would mean for me.

In essence, my dad was even acknowledging that while I could be fearful I should not doubt.

Fear is a normal emotion that God has designed and placed in us to alert us to danger. As we grow and mature physically and spiritually, we become more aware of the alerts. The emotion of fear should not be ignored; rather, it should be controlled. Our response to fear is where we are challenged. In Psalm 56:3–4, it states: "When I am afraid, I trust in you. In God—I boast in his promise—in God I trust, I am not afraid. What can mere men do to me?" The Word of God states clearly that fear will come to us, but when fear comes, we must trust in God. We must have faith. The alert that was taking place was good for me to have in place. The fear alerted me that my transition may cause a gap in my employment, and therefore, I may need to put a hold on some of my spending. Again, I never doubted that God would take care of our needs, but I feared the process. My father was telling me that to operate in this dominion, I would need to do so by faith and not from fear. I could no longer operate with an expectancy that my next steps would come from natural man-driven moves, but they would be faith moves. The story of Rahab and the spies provides an example of the process of moving from fear to faith.

Recognize the Power of God

The first step of moving out of fear and into faith is recognizing the power of God. Rahab gives us the model for exhibiting the emotion of fear and not letting fear control or take over. As the story goes, Joshua sent out two spies to view the land that God had promised them in Jericho. Once they entered into Jericho, they met Rahab. As Rahab encountered the two men, she was fearful of them, not because of what she thought they could do to her but because she knew what the God they served could do. She recognized the power of the Lord: "For we have heard how the dried up the water of the Red Sea for you, when ye came out of Egypt; and what ye did unto the two kings of the Amorites, that were on the other side of Jordan, Sihon and Og, whom ye utterly destroyed" (Josh. 2:10 KJV).

We serve the same God that Joshua served. I know that I, too, have heard about the mighty hand of God, even if I have never experienced these things myself. We need to recognize His power and authority. Our God is the God who rules heaven and earth. Therefore, when we are shaken by fear, we should never doubt that our God will protect us from evil. Instead, recognize that God will make provisions for us and deliver us out of the hands of our enemies. If we are to fear, we are to fear the power and judgment of God, not anything here on the earth. Rahab moved from fear to faith in making an alliance with the one who truly was in control.

Make a Covenant with God

During times of fear, it is important that we follow Rahab's next move and that is to make a covenant with God. It is important that we engage in a partnership with God. Once Rahab realized and acknowledged the power of God by confessing that He was the Lord of Lords, she aligned herself with the right people and engaged in a covenant with God.

> *Now therefore, I pray you, swear unto me by the LORD, since I have showed you kindness, that ye will also show kindness unto my father's house, and give me a true token. And that ye will save alive my father, and my mother, and my brethren, and my sisters, and all that they have, and deliver our lives from death. And the men answered her, our life for yours, if ye utter not this our business. And it shall be, when the*

> LORD *hath given us the land that we will deal kindly*
> *and truly with thee.* —Josh. 2:12–14 KJV

Oftentimes we engage in partnerships with the wrong people out of fear. We make alliances with the people that seem to speak the loudest or have the largest number of outward supporters. The majority of the people in the office, in the community, and even in the church are against the Lord's vision; and therefore, we find ourselves just going with the flow and the majority. Rahab, however did the opposite. I am amazed that in this scripture lesson Rahab began to partner with the two men, versus partnering with the entire city. I guess Rahab knew that if the Lord is for you, then He is more than the whole world against you. God wants us to partner with him. God is telling us that He is all we need. I don't have to operate from a place of fear if I believe that God is going to protect me, even in the times where everyone else is doing the exact opposite of what I am doing. Your faith has to tell you that you deserve His love and protection. God wants to use us to demonstrate His power in our lives.

Find Yourself Worthy Enough to Be Used by God

God really wants to use us to show the world that He is the almighty God. The problem is we think that God can only use certain people. Rahab would be considered as one of the most unlikely people to be used by God. Rahab didn't hold a respectful job; she was a prostitute. However, once she aligned with God's plan, she became a woman of mercy and great faith. God already has a plan for your life, and it is a plan to prosper and not to perish. Rahab knew her worth in partnership with God. Rahab would go on to save not only herself, but she also saved her entire household. She surrendered to God and not the enemy.

Rahab heard what God had done from others. Now she was able to witness for herself what God could do in her life. Hearing about God's power and personally experiencing God's power are totally different. Have you ever heard a word from the Lord for yourself? I have heard a word from Him. There are even times in our lives that when we do hear the voice of God, what God is telling us can actually be scary. The news that is delivered can come with a fear of having to go through the process to get to the promise. I am reminded of the word God had given unto Noah.

God told Noah that He was going to destroy the earth. "So God said to Noah, 'I am going to put an end to all people, for the earth is filled with violence because of them. I am surely going to destroy both them and the earth. So, make yourself an ark of cypress wood; make rooms in it and coat it with pitch inside and out'" (Gen. 6:13–14). I can just imagine Noah hearing this word from God. Even though God told him the plan that He had to save him and his family, he might have thought, "I am fearful. God says He is going to destroy everything but I will get to live. The process is what I fear."

However, Noah demonstrated how to move from the fear to faith. Noah spent 120 years building an ark—all because he trusted God's promise to destroy everything on the earth with a flood. Had Noah been fearful, he may have tried to flee the area, hide, or even give up on the word that the Lord told him. During that time, all Noah's neighbors laughed at him. But Noah never gave up. He continued to build his ark and have faith in the promise of the Lord. He trusted in the Lord; not just for one day or two, he trusted for 120 years.

Noah built and made a covenant with God, partnering with the right side of history.

> *"I am going to bring floodwaters on the earth to destroy all life under the heavens, every creature*

that has the breath of life in it. Everything on earth will perish.[18] But I will establish my covenant with you, and you will enter the ark—you and your sons and your wife and your sons' wives with you.[19] You are to bring into the ark two of all living creatures, male and female, to keep them alive with you.[20] Two of every kind of bird, of every kind of animal and of every kind of creature that moves along the ground will come to you to be kept alive.[21] You are to take every kind of food that is to be eaten and store it away as food for you and for them."[22] Noah did everything just as God commanded him." —Gen. 17–22

Noah continued to move in his faith and covenant with God. In so doing, Noah was able to save his entire family.

God honors those who have faith in his plan for their lives. God especially is there for those who choose to worship him in the midst of danger. The story of the three Hebrew boys, Shadrach, Meshach and Abednego are great examples of moving from fear to faith. Shadrach, Meshach and Abednego refused to worship the golden statue that King Nebuchadnezzar had set as their god.

"Your Majesty has issued a decree that everyone who hears the sound of the horn, flute, zither, lyre, harp, pipe and all kinds of music must fall down and worship the image of gold, and that whoever does not fall down and worship will be thrown into a blazing furnace. But there are some Jews whom you have set over the affairs of the province of Babylon—Shadrach, Meshach and Abednego—who pay no attention to you, Your Majesty. They neither serve your gods nor worship the image of gold you have set up." —Dan. 3:10–13

The three were brought before King Nebuchadnezzar for not obeying. However, instead of being afraid about not worshipping and doing what everyone else around them was doing, they informed the king that their God would be with them. Nebuchadnezzar commanded that they be thrown into the fiery furnace, heated seven times hotter than normal. The boys did not stay in fear because they knew that their God would protect them from the flames. And the God that we serve did just that. In fact, the king, when he looked in to see them, he saw four figures walking unharmed in the flames and the fourth looked "like a son of God." Seeing this, Nebuchadnezzar brought Shadrach, Meshach, and Abednego out of the flames and promoted them to high office, decreeing that anyone who spoke against their god should be torn limb from limb. This is the power of our God. When you go in the confidence of knowing that you serve a mighty God and fear no man, you will be elevated. Shadrach, Meshach, and Abednego went from being tossed into the fire to being promoted to high positions. God used the three Hebrew boys to bring others to know Him and serve Him.

It is not uncommon for the world to try to "put you in the fire" because you don't serve the gods that they serve. Today it may not look like a golden statue or partnering with known enemies. However, it is compromising values, rearranging the focus of our worship, and fearing that if we don't compromise, then we may lose our jobs or have failing attendance in church. We fear that the fire will burn us instead of trusting the process that God will and can use us to show the world that His way is the only and best way. When we can begin to acknowledge God's power, partner with Him, and allow Him to use us, we can move from fear to faith. Walking in faith will take us from hysteria to worship, from a place of distress to a plan of action, from depression to joyfulness, from abuse to love, and from being bound to being set free.

Praise Break

Prayer: Father God, I thank you for entering into every area of my life. Lord, as my faith increases and my fear decreases, I ask that you continue to show me your power in every area of my life. Lord, open my eyes so that I can see that you can use me to save my family, my friends, my neighbors, and my country. Give me the courage to go before strangers and even enemies to do the work that you have called me to do. God, eliminate the need for me to have acceptance of man if it is not your will. I partner with you today, Lord, to be a part of every decision that I make from this day forward. You get the glory, and I get the victory.

Scriptures:

Psalm 34:4:
I sought the Lord, and he heard me, and delivered me from all my fears.

I Peter 5:7:
Cast all your anxiety on him because he cares for you.

Psalm 118:6:
The Lord is with me; I will not be afraid. What can mere mortals do to me?

Psalm 16:8:
I have set the Lord always before me: because he is at my right hand, I shall not be moved.

2 Timothy 1:7:
For God hath not given us the spirit of fear; but of power and of love and a sound mind.

Proverbs 3:5-7:
Trust in the Lord with all thine hear; and lean not unto thine own understanding. In all thy ways acknowledge him; and he shall direct thy paths. Be not wise in thine own eyes; fear the Lord, and depart from evil.

John 14:27:
Peace I leave with you, my peace I give unto you: not as the world giveth, give I unto you. Let not your heart be troubled, neither let it be afraid.

Chapter 8

The Test

◇◇◇◇◇◇◇◇◇◇◇◇◇◇◇◇◇◇◇◇◇◇◇◇◇◇◇◇

"Some time later God tested Abraham. He said to him, "Abraham!" "Here I am," he replied."
—Genesis 2:1

It's time for me to take yet another test. This time, however, the test is actually on what I have written so far in this book. I had the idea of writing this book about a year after my mother-in-law passed away. Doing the math, that would mean that it has been about five years between when the idea came to me to write this book and my actually completing it. I had what many would call excusable reasons: completing my doctorate, raising my children, answering the call to ministry, and a full-time job were just some of the things that deterred the process. This year was going to be different; the book could be the priority, and I could dedicate some time and space to completing the book. I had given myself a deadline to have the book completed. By now I was supposed to be in the editing stage and done. I was on track to do so until my plans were disrupted with my need to have surgery. So, here we go, I am in the midst of my own struggle. My plans were once again disrupted, and may I add, it was rather abrupt.

As most teachers do in the summer time and during breaks, we schedule all of our doctor's appointments, car services, and any other personal needs. I went for my yearly exam in August feeling just fine, and the next thing you know, I am having major surgery in September. There would only be eleven days in between the time I received my surgery date to the actual day of the surgery. One would think that would have been the part that drove me crazy the most, but it wasn't. My doctor presented me with my options and told me to think them over and discuss it with my husband. I am one that if the data supports it, if something makes sense logically, then no matter how hard the road ahead seems, I will attack it head on and move forward. So, in this case, it made sense, and more importantly, it would improve my health dramatically in the future days. I made the decision rather quickly, and the next day, I called my doctor and told him I would like to proceed.

Now I was ready, I was geared up, and while this may not have been in my plans, I could still plan for it. I immediately went to my calendar and determined what time would be best for me to have the surgery. Of course, that was what I would do, and the process sounded like this in my head: Let's see here, there is the surgery and hospital stay, then the six weeks recovery—that equals about seven or eight weeks. Where can I find the most optimal seven or eight weeks? There are some major church events that I want to be a part of. I would like it to be after the choir anniversary and before basketball season because both of my boys will be playing in the regular school year. I also need to be back to work in time for me to prepare my students for their graduation projects. Also, with school. I don't want to be out during the time when grades are due. It would be ideal to have the surgery during one of the major breaks of the school year, but then again, I will need help when I get home for recovery, and I don't want to be a bother to anyone during their holiday seasons. I really thought I could lay out all of my requests, and they would be fully honored. I never considered that the operation room, the surgeon, and the surgical team all had to be available on one day for a scheduled operation that was not life threatening. My surgery was needed, but it was not like the patients needing emergency surgeries or those who needed more immediate attention. I quickly began to realize that there were still parts of this that I couldn't control even if I was mentally in a place of readiness. The time between when I said I was ready until the time they gave me the date seemed like forever. I was in a period of waiting. Have you ever been in a period of waiting—waiting on information, waiting on a diagnosis, waiting for a breakthrough, or waiting on your situation to turn around? Depending on what I am waiting on usually determines the conditions of my mood.

While I Was Waiting

I noticed that during that time, I began to feel irritated for no good reason, almost aggravated in my spirit. I could not move forward with planning if I didn't have the date of the surgery. Once again, I realized that I was still trying to be in control of something that I claimed I trusted God to perform in my life. Did I not think that God knew when the perfect time would be for me to have the surgery? Did I not think that God was ordaining all of this to work out for my good? Did I not think that God already assigned the date, the time, and the location, and it was all going to be what was best for me? Did I not think that God already designed what needed to happen before the surgery, during the surgery and after the surgery? I couldn't believe myself; I was doing it again.

I was so done with my own disposition. One morning during this waiting period, I woke up and said, "I declare that no matter what happens or doesn't happen today, today is going to be a good day." I knew that I had to place a word in my spirit in order to change the direction of my thoughts. The scripture that the Lord placed before me that morning was: "Yours, O Lord, is the greatness, the power, the glory, the victory, and the majesty. Everything in the heavens and on earth is yours, O Lord, and this is your kingdom. We adore you as the one who is over all things" (1 Chron. 29:11). I repeated this scripture throughout the day.

As my day progressed, I owned that I served a God who is everything! So now, while I am waiting, I am not really waiting on the answer or the situation to turn around because my God is, was, and will forever be the answer to all my needs. The date of the surgery is the date that God had designed. When I turned my focus back on my God, I got my joy back in waiting. I was not waiting on a date; I was now anticipating the joy of God manifesting his power, glory, victory, and majesty in my life. As soon as I redirected my mind from the struggle to the praise, I got the phone call the next day that my surgery would take place on September 12. In case you are wondering, it was the very date that I did not want.

The date of the surgery seemed to be placed right before some of the things that I wanted to be a part of: the choir anniversary and my youngest son's first football game as a middle school player. It also gave little time for me to prepare to leave my students for an extensive period of time. I instantly went to a place of how will all of the people around me be affected by my absence? I didn't want anybody's life interrupted because of me. The fact was, I didn't have much time, and at this point, it was beyond my control. Finally, I got to the point where I had no choice but to yield it all to God. I had to fully embrace that God was in control, not me or my plans. I had one job to do now, and that was to stand still and let the Lord do His mighty work in my life.

Stand Still and See the Salvation of the Lord Work

The day of my surgery, my father spoke a word to me right before I was taken back to the operating room. He said to me, "The Lord told me tell you to stand still and see the salvation of the Lord work." Although those words were very comforting to me, it was almost as if I didn't need words of comfort. I was very calm and okay about going in to have the surgery. I don't know if it was because everything happened so quickly that I didn't have time to think about it or research much on the procedure. I can remember telling my husband that I was so tired that I welcomed the rest. This would be my first major operation. The only times I have been in the hospital was for the birth of my children, and even then, I had natural deliveries.

    I was a novice patient and had no idea how I would feel afterward. I had fourteen fibroid tumors in and around my uterus. Many of the fibroids were large in size, some the size of a tennis ball. The fibroids were causing anemia, high blood pressure, menorrhagia, and fatigue. When the doctor removed my uterus, he was able to take a picture. He showed me the picture a few days after the surgery. When he described to me what I was actually looking at, he said to me, "Your uterus was the size of a cantaloupe, and Tiffany, the normal size of a uterus is about the size of an egg. Not only was your uterus vastly different in size, it was also awkward in shape." He continued to say that I was going to feel so much better now that it was removed. Due to the size and the number of the fibroids, I did not qualify for the less invasive form of surgery, such as a laparoscopic hysterectomy. Instead, I had an old-fashioned total abdominal hysterectomy. In general, the biggest difference is that this form of hysterectomy surgery requires a longer hospital stay and recovery time than the others.

    Rest and recovery was the next step and so far the hardest step in the entire process for me. I had become so accustomed to feeling exhausted, functioning with all of the side effects of having fibroids that in my mind, I didn't know that what I was feeling was not normal. My level of activity and engagement was so high that it camouflaged my true health condition. Two things were demonstrated throughout this process: I was doing and going a lot, and I was doing it on fumes. I could clearly see the purpose for the surgery and even the type of surgery, but I could not get ahold of the purpose for resting. Everything before now in my life was a contradiction to what they were saying would lead to a complete healing. How could resting lead to healing and recovery?

The thought and idea of resting and recovery was perplexing to me. In my world, if you don't do, then you don't get. Nothing good could come out of resting beyond the point of natural sleep. I equated rest to being idle. Since when did being idle lead to something good? "An idle mind is the devil's workshop." Everything has to have a purpose, and for me, that purpose needed to lead to productivity, a result or outcome that left something greater than it was before I touched it, partnered with it, engaged with it, and/or experienced it. Resting means that I would not do anything, and here is where my father's Spirit-ordained words would be made real in my life. I was not going to do anything but stand still and see the salvation of the Lord at work.

Resting ended up being more taxing and more productive than I could have ever imagined. I was going through metamorphosis, and this time I recognized that I was in the third stage—the chrysalis. From the outside, it looked like nothing was happening, but on the inside, a lot was going on. I had reached my full weight and length in this spiritual stage of my life and now it was time again for me to wrap myself in the Word (the chrysalis) and let the Lord do all of the work on the inside that needed to be done. It was amazing to me that I could not see inside my abdomen, but, trust me, I could feel that something was going on inside that I had absolutely no control over. My work was to stand still and see the salvation of the Lord work. God was about to do a new thing in my life, and He was using a physical opportunity to do spiritual work. It took me having surgery with a mandate to rest for me to no longer feel guilty about doing nothing.

Operate Out of Your Gift and Not Your Guilty Feelings

Guilt plagued me throughout this process. There were times that I didn't even want to share what was going on with me, mainly because I would think about other people and what they were going through and think this doesn't even compare. I would say to myself: don't waste people's time; this is not worthy of even a prayer request. I felt guilty about not catching this earlier or being able to wait for a later date because I was about to leave my students for seven weeks. Guilt was my overall feeling, and that led to me only wanting to have those visitors I knew understood what I needed without my saying it. I needed people who I knew without a shadow of a doubt could deal with whatever emotion I projected without judgment. I had a strong need to respond and engage with people, and I knew that if I couldn't do that to the level that I thought was appropriate, then I would feel—you guessed it—guilty. In hindsight, I realized that some people may have viewed this as me being a private person, and to some degree I am.

However, in this case, I was more concerned about the level of energy I would need to exude to ensure that those I was in contact with were having a pleasant experience. I did not want to add another task to anyone's day. I didn't want to be on anybody's to-do list. There was just one problem: I needed someone, and it was not realistic for me to think that I would not interrupt someone's plans or day-to-day routine. Then, God did the most beautiful thing. He showed me that those helping me were not operating from a to-do list, and they were not doing this because they were forced to do it. They didn't do this because they would feel guilty if they were not there because they were my sibling, pastor, husband, or friend. They were doing it because they were operating out of love, and they were utilizing their gifts.

God continued to show me that He is God, not only did I have the right person with me at the right time, He sent the person with the right spiritual gift to me at the time that I needed Him to. The last thing I needed was for someone to be around me only out of their guilt. I was already very sensitive to people's time and motives. I have a gift of discernment that can keenly detect the spirit of behavior motivators. Not only that, but the end product and level of impact that a person has who is operating in their gift is exceptionally different from a person who is operating from any other place. I was so blessed to see this manifest right before my eyes. My hospital care was excellent, but there were days that I didn't like some particular healthcare providers. Okay, to be fair, it wasn't really that I didn't like them as a person, I just didn't like what they are making me do on certain days. I felt like the nurse that I had the last day in the hospital was the best. I wonder whether it was because I was feeling better and thought that she was a key factor to the reason that I was feeling better.

    I didn't think the providers who made me get up and walk the day after surgery and the ones who took my morphine drip away were as good or as pleasant. These providers knew what needed to happen for me to get to my ultimate goal of going home. I didn't need the first round of providers to feel sorry for me or to feel guilty about making me get up the next day after surgery. I didn't need them feeling guilty because tears were rolling down my face because it was painful and I was frustrated. I needed them to operate in their gift and have me move forward because if not, I would have a strong chance of getting blood clots and greater problems could arise. During the rest of my first week of recovery, God would demonstrate this even more to me. I knew that my husband and sisters would be my primary caregivers the first week I was at home. I tried to control who would come when, but somehow that need for control left my purview, and they scheduled themselves.

    The day I came home from the hospital was on a Sunday. Thankfully, I didn't have an extended hospital stay, but I did stay the full length of four days and three nights. It was pure bliss to see Fernando pull up in the discharge circle and take me back home. I even remember enjoying that I was in an open space and breathing in a moment of fresh air. The hospital room had begun to feel enclosed, and I welcomed the change of scenery. The choir anniversary was also this Sunday, but as the Lord timed it, I was not ready to be released until after the choir had done their selections. My husband, Fernando, is such a champion that he managed to meet every church obligation that day and still be my knight in shining armor, picking me up right on time. When I arrived home, I was greeted with the smell of a savory Sunday dinner.

Dinner was prepared by my baby sister, Tabitha. Anybody who has ever tasted Tabitha's food would say she certainly has a gift of cooking. She stayed at the knee of my maternal grandmother, Sally Brooks, and was influenced greatly by her remarkable cooking. Tabitha enjoys cooking, and as with any great cook, she loves seeing others enjoy their food even more. I was so happy to see my nieces and brother-in-law having a good time with my boys. Tabitha had created a sense of home and family that brought me comfort and peace. Knowing that I had the emotion of guilt hanging over me, it was acceptable for Tabitha to be here helping because she made it seem like it was a natural part of her day to drive two hours to my house and prepare Sunday dinner for her family and mine. Tabitha was operating in her gift, and while she worked hard, it looked effortless, and she enjoyed the work. What I didn't know was that God had ordained Tabitha to be the first of my four sisters to come and be with me. Tabitha cooked in large quantities, and this time was no exception. I would eat the fresh vegetables that she prepared throughout the week.

Tabitha and her family left, and it was now time for me to go to bed. I asked my doctor prior to leaving the hospital if I would be able to take the stairs, as my master bedroom was located on a floor above where I entered into the house. I was told that I could as long as I gave myself time to rest in between the time I came home and the time I went up the stairs. I was told not to go up and down the stairs; once I was up there, then I needed to stay up there. I had a pretty good experience walking up the steps to come into the house from the garage. I enjoyed eating and fellowshipping with my family on the main level. I stayed on the main level of the house for about four hours. Surely, I was ready and could take the stairs to my bedroom. I told Fernando that I was ready to go up, so we proceeded to the stairs.

I started out and took the first four steps, and the pain was no more than when I had walking. I got about halfway up the staircase, and then suddenly the pain became unbearable. I began to cry, and I was now faced with the challenge of "Do I go back down, or do I keep going up?" During this time, God sent my father-in-law, and although I couldn't see him, I could hear him. He began to tell Fernando to stay with me: "Stay with her, son, just stay with her." I never thought that Fernando would leave me, in fact, he was almost about to carry me up those stairs. I knew he was with me, but hearing the words reminded me that God had sent this blessed man, my husband, to me, and he was staying right there with me, attentive to my every move, feeling every bit of my pain, and wanting relief for me more than I wanted for myself. As I called on the name of Jesus to relieve the pain, I simultaneously gave thanks to Jesus for giving me Fernando. As I prayed and praised, God granted me the strength to continue up the stairs and make it to my bedroom. Fernando was there with me every morning and night, fulfilling the scripture of 1 Peter 3:7 that says, "Likewise, husbands, live with your wives in an understanding way, showing honor to the woman as the weaker vessel, since they are heirs with you of the grace of life, so that your prayers may not be hindered."

The next day the Lord sent my sister, Tonja. I woke up in great pain this first morning when there were no nurses to keep my medication on schedule and there was no adjustable bed. While my own bed felt great because it was not adjustable, it meant that my body stayed in one position all night. If I was going to change positions, then I needed to be ready for it to hurt like crazy. Most of the time, I didn't have the strength to move my body up. Fernando would have to move me if I needed to be moved. Fernando was great at moving and positioning me to a more desirable and comfortable space. He had had previous experience with learning how to move and adjust a person in need due to helping his paraplegic aunt when he was younger.

The second day at home, I would need another person who had this skill as well. Although this was the second day, it was really the first full day at home after the hospital stay. This day required a dynamic person. I needed some of the items that I brought from the hospital to be organized. I still needed someone to help me stay ahead of the pain and take my medicine on time. I needed someone who could also cook and manage the meals that my co-workers, family, and friends were sending. And, I needed someone who could multitask and do it effectively and efficiently. I required so much that day, and I was in way too much pain to articulate what I needed.

Yet again, God knew exactly what I needed and when I needed it. I needed someone with a positive spirit. My sister, Tonja, was always known by the family as the high-spirited one. She is the life of the party. Her personality is such that she can be a comedian, the prayer warrior, serious business women, both liberal and traditional wife and mother, and she somehow can give that to you all at once. There are times when you want to tell Tonja to sit down and focus on one thing. She has had many career paths: banker, phlebotomist, home health aide, and currently, she is one of the best real estate brokers that I know. It did not take me long to see why God had allowed Tonja to have all of those experiences and in particular why God assigned her to be with me on this day. Literally within ninety minutes, Tonja had organized my bedroom, administered my medicine, prepared my breakfast, settled me into the spot where I would sit for the day, and put away groceries that she brought with her.

Tonja took care of me in the most efficient and effective manner possible. She even had time to log onto her work email and help her clients buy and sell their homes while sitting with me. Tonja was operating in her gift, and because she operated best in this capacity, I no longer had any guilt about her being with me today. She continued to do what the Lord had called her to do for the day, and she was still blessed to handle her business during the process.

Finding Balance

The next day was completely unexpected. Tonja was actually going to be with me for two days, but God, being God, sent my Aunt Virginia to me via my sister, Tonja. My father's sister is considered the family nurse. She has a beautiful, sweet, and quiet spirit—just what I needed on this day. I needed someone to speak to me, in a small, gentle voice, words of encouragement that would increase my confidence to try to walk more and even try the stairs. Aunt Virginia knew an important part of healing—and that was finding balance. It was the craziest thing, but the two most consistent things I heard were, "You have to rest" and "You have to walk." "You need to be still, but you have to move." It was the biggest paradox to both rest and move.

I took the stairs, and that landed me in the bed. I lay in the bed resting, and that led to gas pains and the potential of blood clots. The fact of the matter was that I had to do both; the key was to not do one more than the other. I had to find a balance. Finding balance is simply being able to fit everything that I need to do in the proper way. I had to have a mental shift of what finding balance really meant. My original definition of balance was I can do and be everything to all people and meet every need. I would walk the same amount of time that I rested. I misunderstood that I achieved balance when I made all things equal or when I was giving equal weight to all things.

However, that is not the true definition of balance. According to the dictionary, balance is defined as a means of judging or deciding: a counterbalancing weight, force, or influence: mental and emotional steadiness. Now finding balance in my situation made sense; I could not give equal weight to all things. I needed to walk, and I need to rest, but one could be done more than the other. It sounds so simple, but oh, this was so complex.

My Aunt Virginia was successful in showing me what true balance was for this particular day in my life. I was fearful to walk and take the stairs because of how I felt the last time I took them. My Aunt Virginia was fearful that I would sit too long and develop blood clots. We had to find a balance. In order to find the balance, it required us both to let go of our fear and replace it with faith and practicality. I should not be expecting to never get up, and Aunt Virginia should not expect for me to walk up and down the stairs multiple times a day at a steady pace. I don't think that either one of us had those polar extreme intentions, but often our minds lead us to believe in the extreme. I wanted to walk, and I certainly wanted to rest; I just didn't know how to do both without jeopardizing the other. God sent the right person, gifted in showing me just how to balance both.

As God would have it ordained, my Aunt Virginia was visiting with her daughter, my cousin who also lives in Charlotte. My parents had informed her of my surgery and that I was now home from the hospital. It goes without saying that if anyone in the family is sick, she will be there to care for them. If anyone in the community or church is sick and Aunt Virginia can be of assistance, she is there to care for them. She also has a gift for comforting those experiencing grief over the death of a loved one. I was comforted with my Aunt Virginia being here with me; I just never thought that I would be the one that she was attending to. I had heard and seen on the surface level how my aunt responded and assisted in matters like these, but I had never experienced her care firsthand, and what a blessing it was to experience her care. My sister, Tonja, actually picked her up and brought her over to see me. What was supposed to be a brief visit turned into my sister leaving and working with her clients and Aunt Virginia staying with me the entire day.

I could hear my sister and aunt coming inside the house. By that time, my husband Fernando had gotten me up and situated in the family room where I intended on staying for the day. The two of them come in filled with joy, and I could almost hear a sound of anticipation that great things were going to happen with me that day. Meanwhile, I was thankful that they had arrived, but I was not in the same spirit. I actually wanted to be left alone and unbothered. I needed them here to help me do the things that I couldn't do for myself, but again I didn't want to do too much; and they were sounding like they were going to do too much. I certainly didn't want to disappoint them. I wanted to be strong, and while I didn't want to be a bad patient, at this point in my recovery, I would just have had to deal with being all of those things if it required me to do too much.

After the greetings and pleasantries, my aunt began to make these declarations to me, my sister and my husband. She said, "Tiffany is going to walk today, she is going to rest today, she is going heal, and we are going to have a very good day." Now I had no choice; she was way too excited, and she had told everyone that it would happen, and so now I have to do it for my dear aunt. The power of words! I am no longer speaking as a child, and I am fully aware of the scripture Proverbs 18:21 that says: "Death and life are in the power of the tongue: and they that love it shall eat the fruit thereof." I would eat the fruit of the words that I spoke. Aunt Virginia reminded me to say that I am healed. On this day, I walked. On this day, I went downstairs and ate lunch. On this day,

I went back upstairs and rested. On this day, I was one step closer to complete healing. On this day, I found balance.

I was so amazed at how it just happened with Aunt Virginia that before I knew it, I was doing all of those things without even recognizing that I was doing them until they were done. That was when I just came out and said, "Aunt Virginia really has a gift." The end of the work day had come, and Fernando had arrived home. He was going to take my aunt back to her daughter's home, and so I began to thank her for all she did that day. She told me it was her pleasure. She told me that when she was younger, growing up in a large family of eleven sisters and brothers, she worried about them being able to afford health care. She made a declaration and spoke words over her life, saying, "I want to be in the position to be able to help my family if they need to be cared for," and God ordered her steps to become a nurse. At age eighty-two, Aunt Virginia has taken care of generations of her family, and she has done so with excellence and grace.

Throughout my entire recovery process, I saw God utilizing the gifts of others. When you utilize your gifts, you walk in your purpose. This is why many had joy when caring for me; purpose brings about joy and not guilt. For example, my sister, Tracy, is a wonderful interior designer. She follows the trends of fashion and home décor. Her new find was the minimalist lifestyle. She arrived and spent the next two days with me. During this time, she introduced me to the concept of being a minimalist.

In the process of doing so, she would be sure to use plates and glasses that I would normally look at instead of using to serve my food. She would pick flowers from the bushes in my yard and decorate my plates and other areas of the home. She would rearrange or bring out decorations that I already had but would present them differently. In doing this, she reminded me that God has already given me everything that I need. Standing still allows you to take everything in around you. You gain an appreciation for the beauty and the gifts that God has given to you. I was so busy gathering, doing, buying, getting, and even serving that I was not receiving the fruits of my harvest. I didn't need more; I just needed to spend time with what I already possessed.

As I continued to embrace this season in my life, to stand still and see the salvation of the Lord at work, true joy began to wash over me. There were several people who were walking in their purpose, who used their gifts to aid in my recovery. Some would send me text messages with just an emoji that gave me just what I needed. People would send me cards, flowers, meals, candy, candles, books, text messages, prayers, and daily motivations that I knew were given through the Spirit of God because they came just when I needed them. One day, a friend that I met through my church named Rashonda came to visit with me. She came on a week when I was not receiving any guest outside of my sisters. God, being the God of time, knew that I needed to make an exception this time. Even my sisters (who got a break by the way when she came by to sit with me) said to her, "You must be really special because she is not letting anybody come to this house." The fact of the matter was that God let her come to the house.

By this time, my emotions were overflowing. I felt a great deal of gratitude toward all the acts of kindness I had been shown. At the same time, I also felt very helpless and thought that I should be instantly healed. Rashonda brought me lunch, and as we sat down to eat, I begin to bless our food. I started the prayer giving thanks to God for the family and friends that—and I could not get anything else out due to tears and overwhelming thanks that were flowing. Rashonda continued the prayer for me. It was such a powerful moment to experience a friend who is bonded with you in every aspect of your life, but most importantly, connected with you in spirit. When I couldn't pray for myself, she prayed for me.

With tears in her eyes, she sincerely asked what was wrong. I mustered up a response of "I feel like I should be farther along than

I am at this point." And she responded with a question: "Well, how long did the doctor say it would take? I had to pause and even giggled a little because the answer was six to eight weeks, and here I was on week one. Once she realized that this was not a problem, being the gifted medical professional she is, she knew the answer but she made me state the answer out loud so that I could own that this was not really a problem. She flipped the flow. Here would be the reason why God would send her to me on this day. She said to me, "Okay, let's talk about something else, and we will get your mind focused on something other than yourself." She then asked me for my advice on something in education. I was then able to operate in my gift, and immediately I was answering questions, hoping that I was being of value, and yes, I was having fun as it filled my day with joy.

Praise Break

Prayer: God, thank you for the test. The test came so that my faith would be increased, and your glory would be manifested. Thank you for the stillness of today and the days to come, for the stillness will allow me to hear your voice. God, I thank you for helping me find true balance and understanding that finding balance does not come from giving equal parts to all things. I will no longer be fooled by the enemy to believe that giving a little tiny, exhausted bit of myself to everything will ever lead to anything with real commitment, zest, and intensity.

Scriptures:

Deuteronomy 13:3–5 (NIV):
You must not listen to the words of that prophet or dreamer. The Lord your God is testing you to find out whether you love him with all your heart and with all your soul. It is the Lord your God you

must follow, and him you must revere. Keep his commands and obey him; serve him and hold fast to him.

Proverbs 18:16:
A man's gift maketh room for him. (KJV)

James 1:17: (ESV)
Every good gift and every perfect gift is from above, coming down from the Father of lights with whom there is no variation or shadow due to change.

1 Peter 4:10 (ESV):
As each has received a gift, use it to serve one another, as good stewards of God's varied grace.

1 Corinthians 12:7–11 (ESV):
To each is given the manifestation of the Spirit for the common good. For to one is given through the Spirit the utterance of wisdom, and to another the utterance of knowledge according to the same Spirit, to another faith by the same Spirit, to another gifts of healing by the one Spirit, to another the working of miracles, to another prophecy, to another the ability to distinguish between spirits, to another various kinds of tongues, to another the interpretation of tongues. All these are empowered by one and the same Spirit, who apportions to each one individually as he wills.

Romans 12:6 (ESV):
Having gifts that differ according to the grace given to us, let us use them: if prophecy, in proportion to our faith.

Ephesians 2:8 (ESV):
For by grace you have been saved through faith. And this is not your own doing; it is the gift of God.

Luke 6:38 (ESV):
Give, and it will be given to you. Good measure, pressed down, shaken together, running over, will be put into your lap. For with the measure you use it will be measured back to you.

1 Peter 4:10–11 (ESV):
As each has received a gift, use it to serve one another, as good stewards of God's varied grace: whoever speaks, as one who speaks oracles of God; whoever serves, as one who serves by the strength that God supplies—in order that in everything God may be glorified through Jesus Christ. To him belong glory and dominion forever and ever. Amen.

Romans 12:6–8 (ESV):
Having gifts that differ according to the grace given to us, let us use them: if prophecy, in proportion to our faith; if service, in our serving; the one who teaches, in his teaching; the one who exhorts, in his exhortation; the one who contributes, in generosity; the one who leads, with zeal; the one who does acts of mercy, with cheerfulness.

1 Corinthians 14:1 (ESV):
Pursue love, and earnestly desire the spiritual gifts, especially that you may prophesy.

Ephesians 2:8–9 (ESV):
For by grace you have been saved through faith. And this is not your own doing; it is the gift of God, not a result of works, so that no one may boast.

1 Corinthians 12:9 (ESV):
To another faith by the same Spirit, to another gifts of healing by the one Spirit.

1 Corinthians 12:4–11 (ESV):
Now there are varieties of gifts, but the same Spirit; and there are varieties of service, but the same Lord; and there are varieties of activities, but it is the same God who empowers them all in everyone. To each is given the manifestation of the Spirit for the common good. For to one is given through the Spirit the utterance of wisdom, and to another the utterance of knowledge according to the same Spirit.

Chapter 9

God Chose You

◇◇◇◇◇◇◇◇◇◇◇◇◇◇◇◇◇◇◇◇◇◇◇◇◇

> *"But God chose the foolish things of the world to shame the wise; God chose the weak things of the world to shame the strong. God chose the lowly things of this world and the despised things—and the things that are not—to nullify the things that are, so that no one may boast before him. It is because of him that you are in Christ Jesus, who has become for us wisdom from God; that is our righteousness, holiness and redemption."*
> —*I Corinthians 1:27-29*

Finding Your Purpose

Guilt left me when I felt like I had a purpose other than been cared for. Finding your purpose is not as complicated as many think; your purpose is connected to your gift. Your purpose is connected to a need or void that you can fill for others. I know what you are saying, anybody can send a card, there are millions of teachers, I am not the only one that can play the piano, and you are right. But, what I also found was that although everyone that I encountered that week had a different gift, they carried the same Spirit. "Now there are varieties of gifts, but the same Spirit" (I Cor.

12:4 ESV). It was the spirit in which the text, cards, acts of love, and actions were shown to me that made the difference.

When you operate in the purpose that God has ordained for your life, you will do it under the guidance of the Holy Spirit. You will not do it for reward or recognition; you will do it because you are moved to do it by the Spirit. The person receiving the fruits of gifts will feel God's power in it; it will be different than anyone else giving the same thing. Your gift is your gift, and therefore, nobody else can do what God has called you to do. As Christians, we have to own this and be responsible with our gifts. It requires us to listen to God and talk to God through prayer. I pass a church each day, going to my job, and the church normally has quotes or catchy sayings on its church sign. One day, the quote read, "God doesn't call the qualified, He qualifies the called." Once God has called you, He qualifies you with these good and perfect gifts, and they don't leave you. "For the gifts and the calling of God are irrevocable" (Rom. 11:29).

This is why the thing that keeps pulling and tugging at your heart, the one thing that your mind always goes back to and nags at you always appears. In every job position that I have served, I can't help it, the teacher in me comes out. The only difference between a person appearing to have found their purpose and the person who has not is that the one who has found their purpose is walking in their gift. There is a reason that Satan attacks your faith in doing that one thing that keeps pulling at your heart. The reason is that Satan knows that people in the body of Christ need you to operate in your gift. Satan knows that you are the answer to a need. Satan knows that you have a purpose for being on this earth in this season of your life. "For we are his workmanship, created in Christ Jesus for good works, which God prepared beforehand, that we should walk in them" (Eph. 2:10 ESV). God created you with a purpose and a plan in mind, and the world needs you to do the good works that God created you to do.

I realized that the time would never be the right time. I have several degrees and certifications, and there are still moments and times that I don't feel qualified to minister, write this book, teach my students, or sing a song. It is not a question of whether I or any other person in the body of Christ has a gift or a purpose; the question is, will you listen to the voice of fear and doubt or will you operate in your gift? The question is no longer did God call me to do this work; instead you need to be ready to answer the call in the very place that you are in.

Another attack of Satan is that he not only plants a seed that you are not qualified and that you need more, but he also continues to say that what you are doing is not enough. Throughout this journey, I realized that small acts had huge impacts. My complete healing could not come with the one major surgery. My complete healing required the surgery, the daily phone calls, the visits, the dinners, the rest, and the messages. When God tells you to move and you're purposeful in your movement, meaning you are moving under the advisement of your hearing from God no matter how small, God will increase your efforts. Your giving is significant, your serving is significant, and your life is significant. You are enough to make a huge impact on every situation.

My mother, Janice B. Alston, is a praying and praising woman who has been used by God. God gave her the gift of praying healing prayers for people. Ever since she was a little girl, she battled sickness. Throughout her lifetime. she has undergone nine surgeries and birthed six children. Her first major surgery took place when she was just thirteen years old. My aunts and grandparents would tell me that she used to have a place where she went and prayed to God to heal her. I would often hear my mother say, "All I can do is pray." That would be all that God needed her to do.

My mother has what we call a "hot hand," and when her hand gets hot with the Holy Ghost fire, there is a special healing touch that goes onto the person receiving the prayer. Needless to say that my mother's little act of prayer, as she has describes it, has provided major healing to those she touched. God will sometimes use the very need that you have in your life to be the gift that you give to others. I believe that because my mother had to pray so early in her life for healing, she grew in her faith and her gift to pray the words needed to heal others through prayer. When people tell her, "You don't look like what you have been through; you look so good." She responds back with "You are not seeing me; you are seeing the God in me." I actually say the opposite, "I look like exactly what I have been through." I am smiling, praising, and worshipping God because He provided for me, healed me, and performed so many miracles in my life that I just can't help but be this joyful.

Once we begin to do like my mother and use what we have, God will not only bless those whom you serve, but He will provide and increase over your life as well. Let's look at the biblical story of the widowed woman who cried out to the prophet Elisha that she was in so much debt that the creditors were going to make her children slaves. Elisha asked her what she had in her house already, and she replied,

> *"Your servant has nothing in the entire house except for a flask of oil." He told her, "Go out to all of your neighbors in the surrounding streets and borrow lots of pots from them. Don't get just a few empty vessels, either. Then, go in and shut the door behind you, taking only your children, and pour oil into all of the pots. As each one is filled, set it aside." So, she left Elisha, shut the door behind her and her children, and while they brought vessels to her, she poured oil. When the last of the vessels had been filled, she told her son, "Bring me another pot!" But he replied, "There isn't even one pot left."*

> *Then, the oil stopped flowing. After this, she went and told the man of God what had happened. So he said, "Go sell the oil, pay your debt, and you and your children will be able to live on the proceeds."*
> —2 Kings 4: 2-7

She didn't have much but she had the obedience to listen to God's servant and do exactly what he told her to do without question. In return, God took care of all of her needs. Sometimes God calls you to listen before doing. Because she listened, she saved her entire household.

I am reminded of another story of a woman who felt as though she had nothing but a little to give:

> *"As surely as the Lord your God lives," she replied, "I don't have any bread, only a handful of flour in a jar and a little olive oil in a jug. I am gathering a few sticks to take home and make a meal for myself and my son, that we may eat it and die." Elijah said to her, "Don't be afraid. Go home and do as you have said. But first, make a small loaf of bread for me from what you have and bring it to me, and then make something for yourself and your son.[14] For this is what the Lord, the God of Israel, says: 'The jar of flour will not be used up and the jug of oil will not run dry until the day the Lord sends rain on the land.' She went away and did as Elijah had told her. So there was food every day for Elijah and for the woman and her family.[16] For the jar of flour was not used up and the jug of oil did not run dry, in keeping with the word of the Lord spoken by Elijah."*
> —I Kings 17:12-16

The prophets are still speaking to each of us, and they are saying that we have enough. There are enough materials, time, and seeds of gifts in each of us that are enough for God to use and perform miracles. The calling is on our lives. Your calling still has a purpose, no matter if you're sick, hurting, grieving, rejoicing, or recovering. God will stir up the gift and pour you out blessings that you will not have room to receive. If you are seeking to find your purpose, I suggest that you do as Joshua did; he followed the law.

God called Joshua to lead the people of Israel after Moses died, and when he did, He gave him instruction. God told Joshua to follow the law that Moses had written down. "Only be strong and very courageous, that you may observe to do according to all the law which Moses My servant commanded you; do not turn from it to the right hand or to the left, that you may prosper wherever you go" (Joshua 1:7 NKJV). The Law for Joshua was the Bible and scriptures are there for us today. Operating in your gift and purpose means following the scriptures. Joshua prospered in his position because of his obedience to the will and the way of God. In seeking the scriptures about your purpose and your calling, it also pleases God. Solomon demonstrates this for us in seeking God about the calling that was on his life.

When God called Solomon, He spoke to him in a dream. God asked Solomon an amazing question: "What shall I give you?" You have to be a really responsible person when the sky is the limit. Solomon knew God had called him to be king in the place of his father, David, and now on top of that, God was still offering him more. I must admit I would have probably started off by asking God for material things, but Solomon showed a different way. Solomon asked God for wisdom and knowledge so that he could lead the people well.

God was so pleased that he asked for something that would make a difference in other people's lives and not just his own. God, in return, not only made him a wise leader of the people, He also gave him the things he could have asked for and didn't. He gave him riches, peace from all his enemies, and a long, prosperous life. Sometimes we are asking God for the wrong things; we are asking Him for material things as if they are our calling. God knows that we will need material things to fulfill our calling, but it's not our calling. God calls us to help his people. I have a purpose for working with computers, books, churches, and schools. But God isn't concerned with the books, computers, and buildings. God cares about the people that I am reaching through the schools, computer programs, literature, and churches. Whatever God calls you to do, finding your purpose will ultimately serve people. You may make money doing it, but don't think God has called you to make money. He is calling you to serve people, so always be mindful of how to serve others well.

Finding your purpose, answering your call, or operating in your ministry is something that all Christians can do, not just some. Just like Joshua, we will come to know our purpose as we read and meditate on the scriptures. Your purpose will take faith, and just like Jeremiah, you will be restless and uncomfortable until you step out on faith to fulfill your purpose. Just as Solomon, our purpose will be for people, not things. In the same manner, God has gifted each of us, like Timothy, with the abilities we need to live out our purpose. Jesus has told us, "Ask, and it will be given to you; seek, and you will find; knock, and it will be opened to you" (Matthew 7:7 NKJV, emphasis added). Let me encourage you to ask God to reveal His purpose to you. And when He does, resolve to yield to His will and walk according to the purpose that He gives you.

Act Like What You Prepared For

I had accepted that I had a dual call on my life, both teaching and preaching, but accepting your calling and walking in your calling are two different animals. I know that I have purpose and that even my struggle has a purpose that is greater than I can see. I believe that my small acts have a major impact when God enters the process. I no longer need for the world to understand my impact or to measure my impact. "Be careful not to practice your righteousness in front of others to be seen by them. If you do, you will have no reward from your Father in heaven" (Matthew 6:1).

My giving, praying, fasting, studying, serving, and worshipping was all done for my recovery period in private, and it was wonderful. I was free. I was free to be who God created me to be without worry of judgment. If I wanted to cry, I could cry; if I wanted to sing loudly, I would sing loudly. If I wanted to shout standing, sitting, or lying down, I could and I did. And God blessed me with His presence because I sought him with my whole heart, disregarding whether anyone else knew what I was doing in this house by myself. When God's presence entered and surrounded me. He spoke to me and increased my vision and reminded me of the purpose and calling that He placed on my life.

Now it was time for me to act like what God has prepared me to do in this season of my life. I became anxious about entering back into work, church, and the day-to-day activities that I had been doing before I went out for surgery. I was worried because, while I was healed and feeling much better, I was not still 100 percent actively at the place I was before I had my surgery. The other key revelation for me was that I didn't really need to go back in the same capacity that I left. I didn't want to feel the calendar back up with good things, but rather the things that God had prepared me to do.

I thought about what it was like when I found out I was having my children, from the time I knew to the time that they arrived, my actions indicated that I was going to have a baby. I didn't wait until my children were born to start acting like a mother. I changed my eating habits to better care for my children. I didn't plan any travel at a certain point in my pregnancy, knowing that I could deliver during those times. I changed one of my bedrooms into the nursery, preparing for the baby to come home. I made room for the baby, and it was time for me to make room for what God had prepared me for. Now it was becoming easier for me to say no to things that took room away from my baby, from my purpose. I didn't create the nursery, change my diet, and change my travel arrangements for anything else but my baby. However, when it comes to my ministry and my purpose, it is easy for me to switch out what I prepared the space for with something else.

I grew up with a lot of farm-like animals; we had goats, cows, chickens, and several dogs. I respect, love, and have an appreciation for animals. Some of my best childhood memories are with the times I spent with our dog, Trey. If I had Trey in my adult life, Trey would more than likely get a room in my house. What normally happens to me is that things that I love, things that are not necessarily bad or evil begin to come into my house, my room, and my schedule that I didn't prepare the space for. It looks like me preparing the nursery for the baby, but since the baby is not physically present then maybe I could just let something else occupy the space until the baby arrives. As much as I loved my dog Trey and felt that he deserved a room in the house, the fact is I would not have changed my eating habits, created the nursery, and then allowed Trey to take the nursery over before the baby arrived home. The nursery is still there, and the baby could still go into the nursery, but it is not being used as effectively and efficiently as it should be because I allowed something else that I loved to enter that space that the preparation was not intended for.

I realized that I do the same backward thinking when it comes to my schedule. The reason why my schedule gets full with good things is because I am not acting like I have prepared to birth a healthy baby. If I did, I would protect the space and organize my life and my actions to align with the preparations that I have been making. How often do we get the degree, earn the money, and block the time off, but we don't put the degree to its intended use, we spend the money on everything but what we allocated it for, and we use our time trying to either make up for its misuse or crowd it out with additions.

Let's look at the story of Esther. Esther's actions demonstrated that she had prepared to be chosen as a queen:

> *"Before a young woman's turn came to go in to King Xerxes, she had to complete twelve months of beauty treatments prescribed for the women, six months with oil of myrrh and six with perfumes and cosmetics. And this is how she would go to the king: Anything she wanted was given her to take with her from the harem to the king's palace. In the evening, she would go there and in the morning, return to another part of the harem to the care of Shaashgaz, the king's eunuch who was in charge of the concubines. She would not return to the king unless he was pleased with her and summoned her by name. When the turn came for Esther (the young woman Mordecai had adopted, the daughter of his uncle, Abihail) to go to the king, she asked for nothing other than what Hegai, the king's eunuch who was in charge of the harem, suggested. And Esther won the favor of everyone who saw her. She was taken to King Xerxes in the royal residence in the tenth month, the month of Tebeth, in the seventh year of his reign. Now the king was attracted to Esther more than to any of the other women, and she won his favor and approval more than any of the other virgins. So, he set a royal crown on her head and made her queen instead of Vashti. And the king gave a great banquet, Esther's banquet, for all*

his nobles and officials. He proclaimed a holiday throughout the provinces and distributed gifts with royal liberality.
—*Esther 2:12-18*

What would have happened if Esther would have gone in there and did the total opposite of what she had been taught to do when she presented herself to the king? Esther was adopted and was not the same nationality as the others; she was different. Esther knew this, but it didn't matter to her because she did not present herself before the king as though she was not worthy enough to be his queen.

God is telling us through the scripture that the same concept applies to us today; act like what you have prepared for. Walk into the job interview, knowing that you are the best candidate for the position. Walk into this next dimension of your life, knowing that you are ready for the assignment. Take your throne and rule the land in the position that God has prepared for you. "Thou prepares a table before me in the presence of my enemies, thou annointest my head with oil; my cup runneth over. Surely goodness and mercy shall follow me all the days of my life and I will dwell in the house of the Lord forever" (Psalm 23:5–6).

Praise Break

Prayer: Thank you, God, for all of those who walked in their purpose and used their gifts to enhance and enrich my life. God, I believe that you have called me for a purpose in every season of my life. I have a purpose to fulfill even when I am going through sickness, recovery, or in perfect health. God, continue to show me, especially in my weakest moments, places where my gifts will be the answer to someone's needs. God, thank you for using my small things to make a huge impact. Thank you, God, that I will be ready and willing to go forth, making a difference in my home, in my community, in my church, in my profession, and in this world—through the power invested in me by your Spirit. In Jesus's name. Amen.

Scriptures:

Hebrews 2:4 (ESV):
While God also bore witness by giving signs and wonders and various miracles and by gifts of the Holy Spirit distributed according to his will.

Hebrews 6:10 (ESV):
For God is not unjust so as to overlook your work and the love that you have shown for his name in serving the saints, as you still do.

Ephesians 4:7-8 (ESV):
But grace was given to each one of us according to the measure of Christ's gift. Therefore it says, "When he ascended on high he led a host of captives, and he gave gifts to men."

Romans 12:4-8 (ESV):
For as in one body we have many members, and the members do not all have the same function, so we, though many, are one body in Christ, and individually members one of another. Having gifts that differ according to the grace given to us, let us use them: if prophecy, in proportion to our faith; if service, in our serving; the one who teaches, in his teaching; the one who exhorts, in his exhortation; the one who contributes, in generosity; the one who leads, with zeal; the one who does acts of mercy, with cheerfulness.

Chapter 10
Give Thanks and Praise to God

◇◇◇◇◇◇◇◇◇◇◇◇◇◇◇◇◇◇◇◇◇◇◇◇◇

"It's a good thing to give thanks unto the Lord and to sing praises unto thy name, O most High."
—*Psalm 92:1 (KJV)*

What happens when you praise the Lord? When you praise the Lord, you recognize that God is God. When you praise the Lord, you demonstrate your understanding knowledge of who God is in your life. Praise is done in the present. Yes, you do praise God for things that He has done in the past, and some have enough faith to praise God for the things that are going to manifest in your future. However, praise happens in the moment; your praise is right now. Praising God in the midst of struggle and opposition is the ultimate mark that you have an intimate relationship with God. When you praise the Lord, you become a triple threat. The three things that happen are you *acknowledge* the goodness of the Lord, you *activate* your faith, and you bring *awareness* of God's power to others.

Acknowledge

When we praise the Lord, the Psalmist (92:2) declares that we acknowledge that the Lord blessed us with the morning by keeping us through the night. "To show forth thy loving kindness in the morning, and thy faithfulness at night." You acknowledge that God created the moon, the stars and seas. "Oh Lord, how great are thy works!" Nature proves to us that God is so marvelous, from the mountains to the valleys to the depths of the oceans. God the Creator has placed every living, breathing animal, person, and plant in this universe. "Yours, O Lord, is the greatness, the power, the glory, the victory, and the majesty. Everything in the heavens and on earth is yours, O Lord, and this is your kingdom. We adore you as the one who is over all things" (1 Chron. 29:11). Just reading this scripture increases my faith that there is nothing too big or too little for God to handle. As long as God gives me breath to live each day, I have the power to overcome anything that the day brings. A total acknowledgment of God and who He represents in your life is more than acknowledgement of His existence. Acknowledging God means that you invite him into every process and decision that you make. "The Lord looks down from heaven on all mankind to see if there are any who understand, any who seek God." (Psalm 14:2 NIV) God is waiting for you not only to acknowledge Him but to also understand and recognize that everything that takes place in your life is God ordained or God allowed. "I will give you every place where you set your foot, as I promised Moses." (Joshua 1:3 NIV) There is promise connected to your acknowledgment of God and your trust in His leading and ordering your steps. "And without faith it is impossible to please God, because anyone who comes to him must believe that he exists and that he rewards those who earnestly seek him." (Hebrews 11:6 NIV) When you seek God and fully want Him to be a part of every part of your life; God will speak a word and open the flood gates of Heaven's blessings to shower down on you. "You heavens above, rain down my righteousness; let the clouds shower it down. Let the earth open wide, let salvation spring up, let righteousness flourish with it; I, the Lord, have created it." (Isiah 45:8)

Give Thanks And Praise To God

In our acknowledgment that God is God, I think we often don't think that He is the same God that we acknowledge Him to be in the biblical times or worse yet, we think He is God that only gives miracles to others but not me. In actuality, He is the same God but He is moving in the people that are acknowledging Him as the healer, provider, and miracle worker. As God spoke to the people of Israel with the Ten Commandments; these commandments are still very key to a righteous acknowledgement of how God's will is present for our lives today.

> *"And God spoke all these words:*
> *I am the Lord your God, who brought you out of Egypt, out of the land of slavery.*
> *You shall have no other gods before me.*
> *You shall not make for yourself an image in the form of anything in heaven above or on the earth beneath or in the waters below. You shall not bow down to them or worship them; for I, the Lord your God, am a jealous God, punishing the children for the sin of the parents to the third and fourth generation of those who hate me, but showing love to a thousand generations of those who love me and keep my commandments.*
> *You shall not misuse the name of the Lord your God, for the Lord will not hold anyone guiltless who misuses his name.*
> *Remember the Sabbath day by keeping it holy. Six days you shall labor and do all your work, but the seventh day is a sabbath to the Lord your God. On it you shall not do any work, neither you, nor your son or daughter, nor your male or female servant, nor your animals, nor any foreigner residing in your towns. For in six days, the Lord made the heavens*

> *and the earth, the sea, and all that is in them, but he rested on the seventh day. Therefore, the Lord blessed the Sabbath day and made it holy.*
> *Honor your father and your mother, so that you may live long in the land the Lord your God is giving you.*
> *You shall not murder.*
> *You shall not commit adultery.*
> *You shall not steal.*
> *You shall not give false testimony against your neighbor.*
> *You shall not covet your neighbor's house. You shall not covet your neighbor's wife, or his male or female servant, his ox or donkey, or anything that belongs to your neighbor."*
> —*Exodus 20: 1-17*

Interestingly enough, the Word and the Will of the Lord can scare a person. God's voice is so strong, and direct that we are not often ready to directly receive him. "When the people saw the thunder and lightning and heard the trumpet and saw the mountain in smoke, they trembled with fear. They stayed at a distance and said to Moses, "Speak to us yourself and we will listen. But do not have God speak to us or we will die." Moses said to the people, "Do not be afraid. God has come to test you, so that the fear of God will be with you to keep you from sinning." (Exodus 20: 18-22)

Acknowledging God also means fearing Him. We are fearful of those people and things that we will feel have more power than what we possess. If we acknowledge God as being the greatest power, then our fear should lie solely in not doing His will vs. fearing any other being or attack that comes our way. We must have fear that without God there would be nothing. Power belongs to God. When God is in our process, then there are no limitations. Praise becomes an automatic trigger when we sincerely acknowledge

God is God. God is Alpha and Omega, the beginning and ending. Acknowledging God's power and infinite dominion reminds me of exactly who God is in my life, and that increases my faith.

Activate Your Faith

You must never doubt in the dark what God has shown you in the light. Your faith can't be activated until the dark days come. God's light is what will show up in your darkness. Faith requires us to believe that what is not physically present, what is not verbally possible will be fulfilled when the Light of God shines. Without the darkness, the light is not factor. God is a major factor. He has to be a factor in our lives. Jesus came to us in darkness just so His light could manifest to all man. I can imagine Mary and especially Joseph feeling like they were "left in the dark" not understanding that the immaculate conception was able to take place. However, when the Angels appeared, the light appeared. Faith is understanding that God will manifest his light in those times that nobody understands. When you are with God, when you are in God's presence, He will share with you great and glorious things to come in your life. I am reminded of the lessons that Peter taught us when he began to doubt in the dark.

> *"And Peter answered him, "Lord, if it is you, command me to come to you on the water." He said, "Come." So, Peter got out of the boat and walked on the water and came to Jesus. But when he saw the wind, he was afraid, and beginning to sink, he cried out, "Lord, save me." Jesus immediately reached out his hand and took hold of him, saying to him, "O you of little faith, why did you doubt?" And when they got into the boat, the wind ceased. And those*

> *in the boat worshipped him, saying, "Truly you are the Son of God."*
>
> —*Matthew 14:28-33*

Examining Peter walking on water in response to Jesus' walking on water, we learn that his doubt came when he stopped looking to Jesus as the Light. In the beginning of the storm that was surrounding him, Peter looked to Jesus. The problem arose when he stopped looking at Jesus. Peter teaches us that especially when life sends us tumultuous storms, look for Jesus and keep looking to Jesus.

Activating your Faith means that you have to obey the voice of the Lord and take the next step. Peter took one step to get out of the boat and onto the water. Peter was doing just fine when he was focused on the next step, but he got into trouble when he lost sight of his next step. When what is greater is before you, you will go to it. When you realize that getting to your destiny is more important than the moment surrounding you, then you will take the next step and the next step. Obeying God and activating your faith will sometimes look like Peter; you obey God even when it looks like it makes no sense.

When you activate your faith, you allow God to take over. Peter did not experience the supernatural power of God that allowed him to walk on water until he trusted, as evidenced by his actions. Juxtaposed this to when Peter begin to fear, and his faith was diminished. Simple concept but hard action – no faith, you sink, with faith, you walk on water. When Peter had faith, he walked on water. When he had fear, he sank in the water. As soon as your fear takes over, your vision will tank and you will sink. The good news is that Jesus is always there to save and deliver us even when we begin to sink. We know that Peter had a little faith, and a little faith is better than no faith at all. However, you will only go as far as your faith will take you. If I am honest, I, too, am like Peter, depending on

Give Thanks And Praise To God

the situation and the day, I have enough faith to walk on water and then there are moments where my faith relies totally on Jesus rescuing me. The impact of this scripture is that I recognize that there are levels to faith. I am now seeking a higher level of abounding, sustaining faith even greater than my current level of faith.

When you activate your faith, you will immediately go from worrying to worshipping. In an instant, the men went from worrying about their circumstances to worshipping Christ. They begin to praise the Lord because the wind stopped blowing and provisions had been made. The faith level that Peter was on was that he could worship God during the storm. However, his counterparts had to see the deliverance to get to the point of worship. I am not judging them, there were and still are some times in my life that I am relaying on seeing the faith of others for my faith to increase.

Faith comes by hearing and hearing by the word of God (II Cor. 5:17). When you offer up your praise to God, you activate your faith. You begin to put your faith in action. Remember praising God is a right-now event. "I will bless the Lord at all times. His praise shall continually be in my mouth" (Ps. 34:1). In order for me to continually praise the Lord, it requires me to praise God when I am struggling and when I am soaring. Here is what I know: I know that I called on the Lord and gave thanks to Jesus when I was on climbing those stairs, and I felt better. I know that when I praise the Lord, I invite Him to be a part of my struggle, and my faith tells me that we will win and overcome. I know that when I praise the Lord, it takes my mind off of the situation and places it on God. When I praise God, I activate my faith, and therefore, I receive the promises of Christ my King. When I stand on the promises of God through my faith, He fulfills them in my life, and I can't help but to tell someone about my God's goodness.

Awareness

God has been so good to me that I often just want to shout it out loud. There are so many ways to tell of the goodness of Jesus. There is so many venues and platforms now that we can make others aware of what God has done in our lives. It is important that we give testimony because it increases the faith of other believers. More importantly, it encourages the unbeliever to come and have a relationship with this powerful God. It is your public demonstration and witness to others that God is the one who has worked and performed miracles in your life. "And we are witnesses to these things, and so is the Holy Spirit, whom God has given to those who obey him" (Acts 5:32 ESV).

Although we don't often see the traditional testimonial service in our houses of worship, it doesn't mean that witnessing is not still taking place. I have been encouraged by physical actions that I have seen from others. I have been encouraged by Facebook and Instagram posts and Twitter messages. I have been encouraged by those giving their witness to me via text or through a personal conversation. I often say that we need to begin to fill social media and saturate the media and every platform that we have to tell about the goodness of Jesus. It is hard for those nonbelievers to receive Christ if they have no indication of the power and privilege that comes with knowing Him. "Even the Spirit of truth, whom the world cannot receive, because it neither sees him nor knows him. You know him, for he dwells with you and will be in you" (John 14:17).

After my father's surgery, the doctors suggested that he continued with radiotherapy. This is a normal practice for those who have just had surgery as a precaution. "The aim of chemotherapy after surgery or radiotherapy is to lower the risk of the cancer coming back in the future. This is called adjuvant treatment. The chemotherapy circulates throughout your body and kills off any cancer cells that have broken away from the main tumor before your operation."[16] My father had already been a witness to the power of God before his surgery and during the recovery of his recovery period. The hospital staff described him as the most pleasant, caring patient they had seen in a long time. He would constantly ask them about their day and if they needed anything. My father told me that "the greatest witness is through your actions. They will know that we are Christians by our love." My father had prayed about his surgery, and the procedure went extremely well. However, this was only the beginning of how God would use him to witness to others.

My father recalls a time when he was approached by someone who said to him, "You mean to tell me that you are having surgery and you are going through cancer treatments. What are you doing here? I thought you were a faith-walking man. I thought you of all people would have the faith that God could heal you and that you wouldn't need it." As his daughter, this was very irritating to hear. Where I found irritation, my father saw opportunity to witness to the nonbeliever. My father's response to me was that he was not going through the cancer treatments because he didn't have enough faith in God. However, God chose him to go through it so that he could be a witness to the miraculous healing power of God. My father described this particular day to me. "Tiffany, I can still see the moment clear in my mind. I was on the examination table, the medical staff had begun to hook me up to the machines to continue in treatment. A cloud came up and around me, and before I knew it, I uttered the words, "It is complete." The doctor said to me, "You are not coming back, are you?" and I said, "No. I am not." The doctor then told the other medical staff to unhook me. I had all of these lines plugged up to the machines. Tiffany, I am a witness that God can heal. I never quit preaching, I never stopped singing, I never stopped pastoring, I never stopped witnessing because my faith in God told me that I was healed. Yes, God used the doctors and other caregivers to help me in my process, but God was the healer. I was a witness to medial staff, to the nonbelievers, to all those around me."

My father's praise was louder than his struggle. His witness was greater than any trail, tribulation, distress or doubter that came his way. "Yet what we suffer now is nothing compared to the glory he will revel to us later." (Romans 8:18 NLT) The glory of the Lord will shine in our lives and all will see his glory. It is good to give thanks and praise to the Lord because we help to bring light in a dark world. I know that I am a living testimony and that God is using every situation in my life to show the world that He is God.

Praise Break

Prayer: Father God, thank you for giving me the courage to use every platform I have to tell about your goodness and your mercy. God, as I wake each day, let me acknowledge that you are the Lord of lords and that through you, I have the power and victory over the hands of the enemy. Today I activate my faith by recalling to my mind and speaking the promises of your holy Word what you have done and will do in my life. Lord, on this day, I will be a witness to others and make them aware of your goodness and our power. Lord, through my life and through my service, I will use my voice to tell them that you are a Healer, Deliverer, Protector, Wayfinder, and Provider.

Scriptures:

1 Chronicles 29:11:
Yours, O Lord, is the greatness, the power, the glory, the victory, and the majesty. Everything in the heavens and on earth is yours, O Lord, and this is your kingdom. We adore you as the one who is over all things.

2 Corinthians 9:11 (ESV):
You will be enriched in every way to be generous in every way, which through us will produce thanksgiving to God.

Deuteronomy 13:3-5 (NIV):
You must not listen to the words of that prophet or dreamer. The Lord your God is testing you to find out whether you love him with all your heart and with all your soul. It is the Lord your God you must follow, and him you must revere. Keep his commands and obey him; serve him and hold fast to him.

Romans 12:11 (ESV):
Do not be slothful in zeal, be fervent in spirit, serve the Lord.

1 John 4:16 (ESV):
So we have come to know and to believe the love that God has for us. God is love, and whoever abides in love abides in God, and God abides in him.

Hebrews 3:13 (ESV):
But exhort one another every day, as long as it is called 'today,' that none of you may be hardened by the deceitfulness of sin.

Colossians 3:23-24 (ESV):
Whatever you do, work heartily, as for the Lord and not for men, knowing that from the Lord you will receive the inheritance as your reward. You are serving the Lord Christ.

2 Corinthians 9:10 (ESV):
He who supplies seed to the sower and bread for food will supply and multiply your seed for sowing and increase the harvest of your righteousness.

Chapter 11
Praise Reports

◇◇◇◇◇◇◇◇◇◇◇◇◇◇◇◇◇◇◇◇◇◇◇◇

My mother-in-law had a powerful testimony so she formed a cancer support ministry at our church during her journey. After her passing, the ministry would honor her legacy and name the ministry the Fannie K. Little Cancer Support Ministry at St. Marks. The Fannie K. Little support group is still a vital and vibrant ministry. Ironically enough, I have had several of the courageous and strong survivors provide care and encouragement to me during my difficult times. Rashonda was one of them, and Doris was also instrumental in my daily recovery. My mother-in-law realized that there is power in telling and sharing your story with others. She recognized that the power of witnessing and praising God during difficult times give you and all those in your presence strength. I have two powerful testimonies from people who are exemplary models of showing that their praise is greater than their current struggle. These two people are triple threats; they acknowledge the Giver of life, activate their faith, and make others aware of God's goodness.

The first witness is from Kessa Michelle Teasley; she and I have been friends for nineteen years. God brought us together when I first moved to Charlotte. I started teaching at the same school where Kessa was teaching and she and I have shared the joys of being there for each other from the birth of our children to seeing them grow into teenagers. At this stage in our lives, Kessa and I have now shared the struggles that come with health challenges. Not too long ago, Kessa was diagnosed with breast cancer in 2018.

I remember her sharing the news with me, and I wanted so badly to break down and cry. I made myself hold it together. I had to because, frankly, it is harder to cry than not to because she had a spirit about her that said conqueror; and I have never cried tears of sadness because somebody was a conqueror. Kessa knew the God she served, and she walks in that truth. Kessa is another one of those cancer survivors who has encouraged me every step of the way. When I look back on my text messages to Kessa, it was another one of those powerful moments in the Spirit because the two of us were speaking healing, encouraging scriptures, and having chats about our kids back and forth to each other. I was not always the receiver, and she was not always the giver, and those are the relationships that a girl can keep in her life forever. Kessa just doesn't just share the power of her testimony with me, she also shares more globally with others. Kessa gives her testimony on Facebook as she continues to be a conqueror and beat cancer. The following section contains four of her Facebook posts that I know are strengthening and encouraging all those who read them.

When the Battle Is Bigger than You
By Kessa Teasley Stewart

> *"Ye shall not need to fight in this battle; set yourselves, stand ye still, and see the salvation of the Lord with you, O Judah and Jerusalem: fear not, nor be dismayed; tomorrow go out against them: for the Lord will be with you."*
>
> *—2 Chronicles 20:17*

Facebook Post: August 16

The devil thought he had me so many times during my crazy breast cancer journey. The chemo's side effects damaged major systems and bodily functions which caused me to be out of work for 8 of the 9 months of school. But, God kept grabbing me and holding me close, and I never let go! God's GRACE and MERCY kept me! I'm so grateful that I've had a supportive and encouraging village around me. My pastor Rev. Dr. Otto Harris and St. Mark's United Methodist Church family kept me prayed up, and my pastor checked on me and prayed with me regularly. I'm so pleased to report that today I returned to work to start my 26th year in education! My principal, Vincent Golden is da bomb! My school, Northridge Middle, is phenomenal. We are family, and folks can feel that when they visit us!

My journey is still being fought as I continue to recover from the damage caused by the chemo. It's baffling how a drug can kill the cancer and your healthy cells too. The chemo drug nicknamed the red devil has caused the most severe damage. The body usually bounces back. I believe my cancer is gone and that I will recover. I claim the victory and I will continue to praise him in advance! When the chemo devil tries to claim me, I just remind the devil who I belong to and that he can't have me! God's got me! I am his! I'm not sure why I'm going through so much, but I feel compelled to share what was in my heart.

No matter what you're going through, give it to God. Ask him for what you need to get through it. Remember, you are his child and he loves you! He's will not forsake you. Continue to keep me lifted. Thank you again for all of your prayers, donated sick leave, gifts, cards, etc. The living really helped to bless Kyndall and I.

Facebook Post: September 26

> I'm so excited to finally have my port removed today! This port removal represents an end to a traumatic phase of my cancer journey. Continue to keep me lifted as I continue this fight. I will win!

Facebook Post: September 29

> I'll have a procedure done tomorrow to address an issue caused by my chemotherapy. Instead of feeling frustrated over major residual side effects and adjustments I've had to make, I choose to praise and thank God for each day that I am awake! It's another opportunity to grow, work towards God's plan for me, and to appreciate his mercy and love. I refuse to let the devil get the best of me! Thank you for the prayers and texts; it really means a lot.

Facebook Post: November 24

> My oncologist said that I can claim that although there have been issues caused by my chemo and that I'm still recovering from some major chemo side effects, the cancer is gone! The devil can't get me with these side effects! This too shall pass.

The wonderful pastor that Kessa speaks about is the writer of the second praise report that I would like to share. I asked Rev. Dr. Otto Harris if I could share part of a sermon that was preached that highlighted his praise and thanks to God for his daughter's journey. I prefaced my invitation by telling him why I wanted to share his story. I told him that I was wondering how he was able to continue to be a pastor and caregiver of his congregation while he was going through his own difficult time. I never saw the pastor skip a beat. I saw him worshipping and leading others in worship. I saw him praying and visiting the sick. I saw him denying himself and pouring all he had into his congregation during a time when he had every excuse to retreat and tell everyone else to give him space and privacy. Instead, he demonstrated to me how you lead from your struggling place. Trials and tribulations are not just for some of us; they come to all of us. Thankfully, God respects all people and so He is there for all of us in the very capacity that we need Him to be.

How I Got/Get Over
by
Rev. Dr. Otto Harris

◇◇◇◇◇◇◇◇◇◇◇◇◇◇◇◇◇◇◇◇◇◇◇◇◇◇◇◇

My soul looks up and wonders how I'll get over what is troubling me. God has blessed me with a relatively normal life and has allowed me to tangentially experience God's goodness through naming God's goodness to others trying to get over their troubles. I have been walking with others through their application as I applied my theories related to grace, hope, mercy, and faith. As true as it is, I have discovered that in the midst of getting over difficult things, it is not time to discover that "all things work together for the good of those who love the Lord and who are called according to God's purpose" (Romans 8:28). That's not the news to deliver to someone who just received an eviction notice, an unfavorable prognosis, or notification of the unexpected death of a family member.

As pastor, my intent has been to project the spirit of Romans 8:28 upon my loved ones through everyday living so that when an "all thing" that seems unbearable occurs, it is not news but an understanding of how God and life operate. As I have attempted to project this spirit, in theory, God has been projecting it upon me. Through my relatively normal life, I understood and lived by this spirit. Ten years ago, when I suffered a stroke, I believed that my understanding that God would use this as one of the "all things" that would work "for the good." I did not know how my recovery would look. Yet, I got up each day with hope and trust that I would get over.

The theory of the spirit of Romans 8:28 became more real and applicable on a daily basis. From something as minor as trying to make it to the store before it closed or as major as a stroke or preparing to preach my grandmother's eulogy, God gave me peace. I pray that I have been able to extend that peace to others I love. Since my stroke 10 years ago, I continued to "get over" my various challenges in relative stability, until ...

Last summer, during a youth ministry trip, for which I was the keynote preacher, my then 18-year-old daughter's lower extremities begin to swell. My daughter's discomfort was closer to me than a malady to my own body. I felt helpless as I was unable to deliver relief to my daughter. I was thankful that God had my good friend (who was a medical professional) close by to offer relief. I kept preaching. My daughter's legs returned to normal. All things worked together.

Then, my daughter had a couple more incidents of her legs swelling. I knew that was not normal, but I was in a bit of denial and continued my daily routine. Late one evening while home during fall break, however, my daughter knocked on our bedroom door in the middle of the night in excruciating pain. We took her to the emergency room, where we discovered she had fibroid masses. She received medicine to help her control the pain until she could have them removed during her summer break from college. This episode caught me off guard. But, she was at home where she received support and she was able to continue her studies uninterrupted. Again, all things worked together.

That summer, she had the surgery as planned. The surgeon was phenomenal in her preparation. She shared her surgery routine, which included prayer. She had already been praying for my daughter so I could trust her with my daughter's care. The surgery took much longer than we anticipated. I hoped to hear that "I extracted the mass. She's healed. You never have to worry about that again. All things work together…" Instead, we were led into a room where we waited for our surgeon to tell us, "I was able to remove most of it. It took a lot longer than expected, and it has a form that concerns me. I want send it off for testing before we determine next steps." All things did not seem to be working together as I would have wanted them to. I will not pretend that I did not have any anxiety or bewilderment at that time. My theory was being shaken. I believe that I operated, as pastor, as a husband and as a father, out of the overflow of the grace, hope, mercy, and faith that I attempted to project.

I'm glad I already knew and believed that "all things worked together for the good of those who loved the Lord and who are called for God's purpose" because it would have been a horrible time for me to receive that message for the first time. Shortly after I received the news that my daughter was not completely healed through surgery, the test results were returned—CANCER. I felt worse than I have ever felt in my life and I had to preach in two days.

I HATE CANCER—there is no battle more intense, immediate, and personal than responding to an attack on a person's body. I didn't know a whole lot about cancer other than it scared me. As I look back three years before my daughter's diagnosis, I recall an experience in which my family was "cancer adjacent." We took a family trip three years ago. I found a cozy suite with plenty of room for the whole family for a phenomenal price. I was a hero for a day.

When we arrived at the suite, I noticed it was in close proximity to what seemed to be a hospital; it was actually in the same parking lot. We checked into what seemed to be a serene atmosphere with medical equipment everywhere. I discovered that I got a great deal at a hotel intended for family members of the patients of the adjacent cancer research center. I was very uncomfortable to say the least. I felt guilty for being healthy and my whole family being healthy. I'm sure the pity that I had in my head and heart was pronounced through my eyes, "there, but for the grace of God, go I." Body pitying is close kin to body shaming. Lord, forgive me. Now, I was in a similar situation as the families in that serene hospital. As I traveled to and from various medical facilities, I felt the pity of those I encountered. I sensed it from some when we went into these medical centers. I sensed it from some of my colleagues. It's that kind of body pitying that kept some from sharing my journey with others and receiving God's grace through support of others around me.

The grace of God that was with me at that hotel (giving me a great price) is the same grace that was with those families, who were fighting against cancer. Once I realized that, I had the good sense to share my journey with those I loved. I was grateful for the same grace that was further extended to my family from our family and friends—that superseded the body pitying that I loathed. My loved ones saturated my family with concern and sympathy, supplanting whatever pity I mistakenly perceived. I was inspired by the stories and encouragement from others who had survived and overcome cancer. I was grateful for those who still treated my baby girl like the "princess" diva that she is. My soul looks back and wonders ... there, with the grace of God, went us.

My daughter kept fighting through pain and inconvenience—which further inspired me. I consider those who have overcome cancer to be heroes—whether through this life or through the life to come; through whatever processes/treatments used whether it be radiation, chemotherapy, surgery, natural treatments, etc. I honor them and praise God for being with them through their journey. We visited with medical professionals throughout the state—gynecologists, gynecological surgeons, gynecological oncologists, urologists, geneticists, chemotherapists, and a radiation therapist. My daughter's situation reminded me of the woman described in chapter 5 of the Gospel According to Mark, who "suffered many things from many physicians" (Mark 5:26). Each doctor that my daughter encountered seemed to add their bad news to the others' bad news. They thought that she might need radiation, chemotherapy, surgery, or even a stent with an external bag. My hope, was, at least (or maybe at most), that she would be okay. But my church family continued to offer support and prayers that seemed illogical to me, such as, But my church family kept offering the most illogical ridiculous prayers and support like, "I pray that her life does not suffer any interruptions. I pray that she maintains that same glow and presence that she has now. I pray that what God is doing will confound the doctors."

After exploring all of the possibilities with the doctors, my family waited on a final test on the genetics of the mass to discover how aggressive it was. The doctors were particularly looking for the "YWHA" gene. If the YWHA gene was present that would mean that the cancer was aggressive and that the treatment would need to be aggressive such as radiation, chemotherapy, stents, or surgery. We received the result: YWHA was NOT present, but YAHWEH (the I AM Who I AM) was present—was always present and will always be present.

The cancer was not as aggressive as it could have been, and my daughter's treatment plan would be primarily through hormone therapy. Hallelujah! I was grateful for good news following all of the bad news. My daughter continued to fight, my loved ones continued to encourage, and we continue to get over. I knew and know that regardless of the outcome that all things would work together for the good of those who loved the Lord and who are called according to God's purpose. My soul no longer wonders how we got over this experience or how you will get over your experiences. YAHWEH, who is always present, helps you get over.

Mary's Testimony

The next two praise reports would not initially be categorized as praise reports. However, when you begin to understand who we are in Christ and are able to reach the level of spirituality of these two next individuals, you, too, will find these to be powerful testimonies. These praise reports give credence to how one can overcome the death of a parent and the death of a child and still praise God. These two individuals provide a shining bright light of hope in what I imagine to be the darkest of times.

The first praise report was given to me by Mary Mitchell Smith. Once again, the Lord placed me on a divine work assignment. This time it would be at a high school, and my second time back as a classroom teacher. I would be teaching at the school that Mary was assigned. We didn't initially meet as colleagues; we met through her role as the high school basketball team coordinator. My oldest son, Camren, was a rising freshman, eagerly interested in the basketball team. A mutual friend gave me Mary's name to contact about the basketball program. I left the conversation with the coaches to his father, and I took care of the paperwork.

Mary also had a son who was playing on the team. Our children happened to have attended the same middle school, but there was a two-year difference between the two of them. Camren would go on to make the basketball team, and therefore, Mary and I would become more connected. I noticed that Mary had a genuine interest in all of the athletes, not just her own son. She cared deeply about their academics and their social and emotional states. In my opinion, she was beyond the "team mom" status. Team moms organize the team meals, serve as the liaison between coaches and players, and gather the required paperwork. Mary was more than this; she did and still does all of these things (even though her son is now playing in college) with an extra special level of care and support.

Once I joined the faculty, I was also able to see Mary engage with her students in this same manner. She is doing more than teaching her students math; there was this extra layer of deep support to her students.

One day, Mary and I were waiting for our sons to come out of practice, and she began to share her testimony with me. I believe we began to speak about this particular time in her life because I asked her if she remembered a student who had shared with me that she was once their teacher. Of course, the student found her to be one of their most memorable and supportive teachers. Initially, Mary was not able to recall the student just by the name I had given her. Later on, in another setting, we would be able to place the name with a face, and she did remember the student. In my effort to get Mary to remember who the student was, I gave her the time frame that the student would have attended the school. When I did that, I saw Mary look down and away, and she shared with me this story. She said:

> I really don't remember a lot about that time in my life. I was in a very dark place. I had a daughter whose name was Meghan, and she died shortly after her second birthday. When Meghan died, I was here, but I was not here. Meghan was born with no indication that she would have such a short life here on earth. I didn't notice that anything was wrong until she reached twelve months old but was still not walking. She seemed to be behind in the fine motor skills and other progress checks for the twelve-month milestone. This caused her medical team to order several tests to see what may be causing her delay. After going through several trials and hospital visits in Charlotte, Duke University, and Atlanta, Meghan was diagnosed with a very

rare immune deficiency disease. I decided to be a part of a case study in Atlanta. Part of the study included gathering my family medical history. Both my husband and I would be tested to see if we carried a gene that would yield this form of disease in our children. However, before the test results came back, Meghan was identified with this virus. She kept getting sick and would never rebound from it, and finally, she passed away. Meghan never looked sick; she never had any of the physical features of disease like the other children. It was always my thinking that she would just get better eventually. I was in such a bad place that my family and friends would lay their eyes on me to see what I was doing in her room by myself. I don't remember the days; I went totally numb. My firstborn baby girl was no longer with me, and I had tried everything to keep her here and care for her. About two months later, I became very sick. I went to the doctor, and to my surprise, he told me that I was pregnant.

The news of being pregnant was shocking enough, but it was the next piece of information that really got me. At the time that they determined that I was pregnant, the test results for me being a carrier of the gene that ultimately caused Meghan's death were not back yet. I can only assume that, given my emotional state and the trauma of just having a child die, many felt that the doctor was in order for asking me if I wanted to terminate the pregnancy. I was totally appalled! I didn't need to consult with anyone; I didn't need to think things over. It was an instant no for me. I had faith that God would keep and protect this baby.

The circumstances of that day said "terminate the pregnancy," but there was another day coming that would say something differently. When I was seven months pregnant with my son, Matthew, the test results finally came back that would determine if I was a carrier of the gene. Remember, my pregnancy with Meghan was normal, and so it was no comfort to those around me that just because I was seven months pregnant that a healthy baby would be born. But God revealed that my test results showed that I was not a carrier of the gene. If I would have operated in fear, I would not have the gift of my son, Matthew. Matthew made me wake up. I became alive with him. Matthew gave me life. I knew that I had to take care of this baby boy. I had to be present for him, and I am glad to say that I have been there for him every day of his life going forward.

I stood in awe of how God could take her darkest hour and turn it into her brightest day. Mary's praise report demonstrates that God can operate and control our lives even when we feel all hope is gone. God moved when she couldn't move. God is always working in our lives, and Mary reminded me that the sun will shine again. I have often heard that the death of a child is extremely difficult because it seems "out of order" because children are supposed to bury their parents. I don't think that either is easy. The death of any loved one cannot be leveled by which hurts the most. The loss of a person's life at any age causes one to grieve.

I have often witnessed others trying to offer their support to others who are grieving, and immediately I become concerned by what I hear them saying in the spirit of comforting words. It's not simply comforting to hear that your mother or child is in a better place now, or that it was just their time to die, or that the person lived a good long life. While these things might be true, we can't and shouldn't globalize or make generic the effect death has on a person. When my mother-in-law passed away, my husband shared with me that he felt like a huge piece of his life was gone. I understood what he was saying, but the feeling of that was too heavy for me to even imagine. He is walking, talking, and working, but he is doing all of these things while feeling incomplete. There were no words I could say to fill that void. Therefore, I learned to stop trying to fill the void of his mother, and instead, I focused on being the best wife that I could be to him. Oftentimes, that would mean not saying anything and just listening. When I didn't know what to say or do, then I would pray for him and our family. To me, praying and listening are the most powerful tools of support.

The Lord would grant me another opportunity to see the power of prayer and how God can restore unto us a peace that surpasses all understanding. The next praise report is from my husband, Fernando. He gave this message to our church family five years after the passing of his mother.

Five Lessons Learned from Fannie K. Little
by
Fernando G. Little

◇◇◇◇◇◇◇◇◇◇◇◇◇◇◇◇◇◇◇◇◇◇◇◇◇◇◇◇◇◇

I don't get a chance to say this often, but I am extremely humbled, grateful, and blessed to have the opportunity each and every Sunday to serve as your Minister of Music. Just like you, I rejoice because we serve a risen Savior who thought enough of me and you to sacrifice his life so that we can have everlasting life. That's something to sing about, play about, and shout about. I could not imagine doing what we do here anywhere else—thank you for being the church for me.

I would also like to thank the Fannie K. Little Cancer Ministry for allowing me this opportunity to share with you. This is the first time that I have spoken publicly about my mom's death and what I have strived to learn from it and more importantly, what God gave me that also included a peace that surpasses all understanding. Even with that peace and even with it being five years since her passing, I still miss her, which is why I may try to move through this quickly, so I can make it through it. Please pray with me.

As I said earlier, I love being the Minister of Music here, which means that the only preacher that lives in my house is the one and beautiful, Dr. Tiffany Alston Little. She can't really help it she's got preacher blood running all through her—her dad is a Baptist minister, her brother is a Baptist minister, and she has uncles and aunts that are ministers of the gospel. It's running all through her. Camren is not far behind because he also can lay down a prayer. If something is on his heart, he will pray a prayer like the Chairman of Deacon Board. To be clear, I am not a preacher. I just wanted to do something to honor the legacy of my mom and hopefully offer a word of inspiration to someone else.

I am glad to see family here today. Thank you for coming. It didn't take much to see that family was important to Mom. She often brought us together through her good cooking. Who remembers her chicken and rice casserole? Red velvet cake? Honey bun cake? Taking care of family was a priority for her. She showed unconditional love and never stood in judgement. She recognized that in Proverbs Chapter 12, Verse 7, that family of the godly stands firm. She knew that family togetherness and family relationships were important to God. That's why her house was the gathering place for Christmas. She was a nurturer and a caregiver to her entire family.

Two weeks before she passed away, she asked Tiffany and I if the boys could go with her and Big Daddy to their spot in Hilton Head. Normally, that would be a tall order for Tiffany to let the boys go anywhere without her overnight. While there were no signs at the time that Mom would not be with us two weeks later, something down inside Tiffany said, "Let them go." The boys had the time of their lives. According to Big Daddy, even though it rained some of the time, Mom and the boys would run out to the beach every time the sun broke through. He said in five minutes they would run back in soaked and wet because it would start raining again, but they didn't care. They came back from Hilton Head on my birthday and mom's hair had grown into this impressive afro. I asked what happened and that's when Big Daddy told me about the beach and the rain. Mom was so happy. That was the best decision to let the boys go with them and little did we know that it would be her last trip. The first lesson from Ms. Fannie that I offer—family togetherness is a Godly priority.

Mom's cancer journey was an explosive one. When things happened, they happened quickly and definitively. She was determined to keep up with everything. She was diagnosed with an aggressive form of breast cancer. It was also inflammatory—which meant that even if a tenth of a centimeter of a cancerous cell was released into her lymph nodes—the cancer would immediately spread to other parts of her body. Mom was always a scholarly student, and she quickly became a student of her own pathology. She started a journal that chronicled her entire treatment process. She noted everything that her medical team gave her and then would research their findings on her own. She participated in an advanced clinical trial and medication regiment that had been reported to produce results with this type of aggressive cancer. We were often asked if we were going to seek a second opinion. Mom knew she had a strong medical team because she questioned them and questioned them and questioned them. When I was in Asheville working at Mission Health she would ask me to forward e-mails to our chief oncologist. Pretty soon she had developed a relationship with that cancer team as well. She was very involved in her treatment process, which in turn caused her providers to stay on their toes and pursue the strongest clinical outcomes for her. She experienced strong outcomes after her first treatment and came very close to a complete remission when her prognosis was that she could have been gone in six months. After six months, she was in remission.

She was educated, and we were encouraged. The second lesson from Ms. Fannie is lifelong learning is important, especially education about your health. I encourage all of our cancer patients and cancer survivors to stay engaged and keep your medical team on their toes. Your engagement will produce a stronger patient experience and strong clinical outcomes.

After Mom's first round of chemotherapy, she and Dad drove up to Asheville for the weekend. She wanted to get away. She was also anticipating the first effects of the chemo—losing her hair. I was glad she wanted to be with us during that time, but at a time when Mom should be the one being comforted, she would always manage to be the comforter. For example, she would only talk about her cancer when she felt that we were ready and that we wanted to talk about it. As she started to lose her hair, she would never let me see it because she thought it would upset me. When she came around me, she would wear her wig. Occasionally, she would ask me if I wanted her to take the wig off. Most of the time, I would say no and she would oblige. She was definitely a "protector" during her cancer journey. She guarded our feelings more than we ever could have protected hers. If she felt serious pain—we never knew it. The most she would say is that she was tired and that's it.

That's how mom operated in the church too. She always put the feelings of others before her own. She always remained cool and calm. She was never irritated. Her welcoming and giving spirit had a tremendous impact on everyone she met—even new members. I've had several new members come up to me and say your mom was the best "first impression" I have ever received from a church. In my mind, she brings Philippians 2:3 to life—"Do nothing from rivalry or conceit, but in humility, count others more significant than yourselves." I try my best to uphold this part of her legacy. Be giving, selfless, and always rejoice, even in the midst of my struggles. Thus, I offer the third lesson from Ms. Fannie—people will forget what you said to them, maybe even what you did to them, but they will never forget how you made them feel.

After her first remission, there was a partial recurrence several months later. Mom's spirit was still higher than ever. I remember going to her job after the news of her second partial remission. She had a "glow" about her that I will never forget. It was more than a glow of beauty. It was an angelic glow and a peace, like she was "covered." Like she was ready for anything, come what may. I remember that all I could say that day was Mom, you look really good. And she said, Fernando, I feel really good.

During the last week in June of 2012, I went to a follow-up appointment with my Mom. She had notified the doctor of a swelling that was happening in her stomach and the doctor ran some tests. He was to give her the results at this follow-up appointment. She asked me if I would go with her. The results weren't good; the cancer was back. Mom took the news well—which made me take it well. She was of the mindset—we've sent this thing into remission before, let's go again. The doctor told her, I am soliciting the help of the entire oncology team this time to find a solution. We left that appointment anxiously awaiting next steps from the doctor.

Mom wanted to go to lunch after that appointment. So, we went to Firehouse Subs. Over lunch, she intentionally brought me up to speed on some of her financial affairs including some provisions she had made for Camren and Chandler's college fund. She also told me that she was pleased with her journey, but that she was not afraid of death. She then followed that statement with—"As long as I have breath in my body, then I am going to fight, you've got to fight! I've got too much I want to see. I want to see my grandsons grow up. I want to be there for them." I said I understood and we finished our lunch.

Over the next couple of days we took mom to CHS-University to have the fluid on her stomach drained. Mom never complained or seemed to be in severe pain. She was not eating well and she was not moving as fast, but she was home. During this time, I was working with her doctor's office to get her next chemotherapy appointment scheduled and she was encouraging me to get that appointment scheduled.

July 5th was a rough day. I had seen Mom the night before at home and she seemed really weak which, of course, was hard to see because she had never been this weak before during her journey.

She never even needed a hospital stay. She had been so strong—we almost didn't know how to handle seeing her this weak. Tiffany went to check on her while I was driving to work. I will never forget while I was on the phone with her doctor's office, Tiffany was beeping in to tell me she had called the ambulance to take Mom to the hospital. She needed to know which hospital to take her to. I said CHS-University because they had just seen her the day before to drain the fluid from her stomach. They should know what's going on. So, I start driving to CHS-University and of course, the knee-jerk reaction was to call grandma. Grandma, Annie Little is the treasure chest of wisdom for our family. I needed to hear her tell me that I was doing the right thing and that everything was going to be okay. I called her and really couldn't get anything out, but in her wisdom, she knew what was happening and she knew what was going on. She helped me get word to my dad at work and other family members.

I arrived at the Emergency Room not really knowing what to expect. Their initial examination did not seem to be too alarming. However, within 30 minutes, I was met in the hallway by the head of trauma surgery whose first words were not hello, how are you, or can I have a word with you—they were, you know your Mom is not going to make it. He said I don't expect her to make it out of the ED. I found myself saying, "I don't know what you're talking about, but you need to ensure that as long as my mom has breath in her body—your team needs to do everything they can do. And I'm serious."

He knew that I was serious. And they did work on my mom. And she fought just like she said she would. She made it out of the ED to a regular room proving the doctor wrong. It didn't take him long to figure out that we didn't have a clue of what had been found in the last tests. The cancer had spread to a significant portion of her internal organs—kidneys, stomach, liver, intestines. He apologized for his demeanor and offered his medical prognosis, which was not good.

At this point, I was able to go in and see Mom. She was coherent, but not able to open her eyes. When she heard my voice, I could see her trying to open her eyelids. She was trying so hard to respond. All I could say to her was that she was so strong and that I was so proud of her. The next day, as her organs began to shut down, they approached my dad and I about starting to relieve her from some of the machines. We were in no position to make a decision on that. In her protective spirit, she relieved us of that burden. She passed away moments later.

The last two lesson that I offer from Ms. Fannie is that it's the Holy Spirit's job to convict, God's job to judge, and our job to love! Mom was always able to turn the other cheek when people disappointed her or let her down because she knew that God had the final say on all judgements. I think about how mad I was at the doctor, and now I am the head of human resources for CHS-University. I now have direct influence over how providers communicate to patients. Look at how God works.

You can probably guess my last lesson. As long as you have breath in your body—you are here for a reason and you shall live for your Lord and Savior! Praise God through your struggle and watch your blessings multiply. Living for the Lord has earned Ms. Fannie an eternal seat in Glory! And it has earned me another angel in Heaven to watch over me. I ask for it quite often. Thank you, Lord ... because you've been good to me.

Praise Break

Prayer: Father God, I thank you for every testimony. God, I ask that you provide every reader with insight surrounding their current situation. Oh Lord, bless those who need to see your glory and your healing power. God, I pray for every cancer patient, caregiver and survivor; may your will be done in their lives. God, let us continue to go into the dark places and the dark hours with an assurance that you will show forth your light and a testimony will form out of our lips. I pray that we become bold and courageous witnesses of your goodness. I pray that we seek opportunities to serve you by serving others. We recognize that without you, nothing is possible but with you, all things are possible. Thank you, God, for never failing us. Thank you, God, for revealing yourself to us in ways that we have never seen before. I pray that as we continue to share your goodness and your mercy that those who don't believe may be able to experience the fullness, joy and hope that come with knowing and abiding in you. I pray for increases in areas of our lives that are desolate. I pray for strength in our weakness. I pray that an influx of peace and positivity overtake our thoughts and daily encounters. I pray for divine connections, opportunities and appointments. Father God, I pray that we come to know you as the God that is Spirit, Life, Infinite, Immutable, Truth, Love, Eternal, Holy, Immortal, Invisible, Omnipresent, Omniscient, and Omnipotent. In the mighty, matchless name of Jesus, I pray. Amen!

Scriptures:

Job 22:21
Acquaint now thyself with Him, and be at peace: thereby good shall come unto thee.

Jeremiah 9: 23-24
Thus saith the Lord, Let not the wise man glory in his wisdom, neither let the mighty glory in his might, let not the rich glory in his riches: But let him that glorieth glory in this, that he understandeth, and knoweth Me, that I am the Lord.

Hosea 6:3
Then shall we know, if we follow on (in the path of obedience) to know the Lord.

John 7:17
If any man will do His will, he shall know.

Daniel 11:32
The people that do know their God shall be strong.

My Praise Report

I would like for you, the readers, to have a place to write your own testimony of how your praise is greater than their struggle. Please use this space to write it down and share it with others.

Endnotes

1. The Editors of Encyclopedia Britannica, "Water Cycle," Encyclopedia Britannica (Encyclopedia Britannica, Inc.), accessed October 23, 2019, https://www.britannica.com/science/water-cycle

2. The Editors of Encyclopedia Britannica, "Water Cycle," Encyclopedia Britannica (Encyclopedia Britannica, Inc.), accessed October 23, 2019, https://www.britannica.com/science/water-cycle

3. The Editors of Encyclopedia Britannica, "Water Cycle," Encyclopedia Britannica (Encyclopedia Britannica, Inc.), accessed October 23, 2019, https://www.britannica.com/science/water-cycle

4. Antanaityte, Neringa. "Neringa Antanaityte." (TLEX Institute.) Accessed October 23, 2019. https://tlexinstitute.com/how-to-effortlessly-have-more-positive-thoughts/.

5. "Emotional." Out of Pocket Emotions offers Individual and Group Life Coaching, May 16, 2016. https://outofpocketemotions.com/emotional-life/.

6. "How Trees Survive and Thrive After A Fire." National Forest Foundation. Accessed October 23, 2019. https://www.nationalforests.org/our-forests/your-national-forests-magazine/how-trees-survive-and-thrive-after-a-fire.

7 Dewey, John. Experience and Education. London: Macmillan, 1975.

8 ChildTalk. "How Many Words Should My Child Be Saying? A Quick Guide to Vocabulary Development," January 1, 1970. http://www.talkingkids.org/2011/07/how-many-words-should-my-child-be.html.

9 Risley, T. R & Hart, B. (2006). "Promoting early language development." In N. F. Watt, C. Ayoub, R. H. Bradley, J. E. Puma & W. A. LeBoeuf (Eds.), The Crisis in Youth Mental Health: Critical Issues and Effective Programs, Volume 4, Early Intervention Programs and Policies (pp. 83–88). Westport, CT: Praeger.

10 Ruston, H. & Schwanenflugel, P. (2010). "Effects of a Conversation Intervention on the Expressive Vocabulary Development of Prekindergarten Children." Language, Speech, and Hearing Services in Schools (41): 303–313.

11 Ruston, H. & Schwanenflugel, P. (2010). "Effects of a Conversation Intervention on the Expressive Vocabulary Development of Prekindergarten Children. Language, Speech, and Hearing Services in Schools (41): 303–313.

12 Ruston, H. & Schwanenflugel, P. (2010). Effects of a Conversation Intervention on the Expressive Vocabulary Development of Prekindergarten Children." Language, Speech, and Hearing Services in Schools (41): 303–313.

13 "Butterfly Life Cycle: Article with Lots of Pictures.". Accessed October 23, 2019. https://www.thebutterflysite.com/life-cycle.shtml.

14 "Butterfly Life Cycle: Article with Lots of Pictures.". Accessed October 23, 2019. https://www.thebutterflysite.com/life-cycle.shtml.

15 The Exodus Route: Pi-Hahiroth. Accessed October 23, 2019. http://www.Bible.ca/archeology/Bible-archeology-exodus-route-pi-hahiroth.htm.

16 "General Cancer Information." When you might have chemotherapy | Cancer in general | Cancer Research UK, January 17, 2015. https://www.cancerresearchuk.org/about-cancer/cancer-in-general/treatment/chemotherapy/when-you-might-have-chemotherapy.

CPSIA information can be obtained
at www.ICGtesting.com
Printed in the USA
LVHW082006170420
653851LV00019B/1775